TO CH

I Hope you enjoy
the book !

Damian
Donati

AIRPORT

GUN

DUDE

AIRPORT GUN DUDE

DAMIAN DONATI

Deeds Publishing

Published by Deeds Publishing in Athens, GA
www.deedspublishing.com

Printed in The United States of America

Cover design by Deeds Publishing

ISBN 978-1-950794-44-7

Books are available in quantity for promotional or premium use. For information, email info@deedspublishing.com.

First Edition, 2021

10 9 8 7 6 5 4 3 2 1

I have been writing for over 26 years, but never really took the time to take a writing to publication, until now, with this book. This 7 year effort is dedicated to my wife, Wanda, who I dated in high school, and who I married 37 years ago. She was always pushing me and telling me, "You need to finish a book!" She supported my reading this book and other book drafts to her for hours on end while we were both in laughter and in tears. She put up with my hours, days, weeks, months and years, while I focused on finally finishing this effort.

Thank You, Wanda!

PREFACE

He has never been in any trouble with the law in his entire life. One beautiful summer morning, as he was embarking on a fun filled company trip to Chicago to party and attend a Cub's baseball game, he unknowingly made a terrible mistake. Due to this oversight, he was arrested and subsequently sent to jail. This was a total shock to him, his friends and his family.

This wasn't just any jail though; this was the Clayton County Jail in Clayton County Georgia. For those that live in metro Atlanta they know that Clayton County is the county most notorious for crime. Those watching the local nightly news know that Clayton County is mentioned often in the crime reports. While the author is from the north Atlanta suburbs, the jail was in the "hood."

He was very unsure about his trip to jail, even scared. But as the experience unfolded he learned that jail wasn't so bad after all. He learned how to laugh with his cellmates, listen to their unique stories, learn from them, as well as teach them lessons that they likely had never been taught.

His unexpected humorous and emotional experience in jail will teach all readers that we all can enjoy one another and laugh with one another, regardless of our backgrounds or economic statuses. This book tells a very enlightening, funny and serious story of his jail experience bringing laughter and even tears to the reader, as he describes his experience in the Clayton County Jail.

IT WAS SUPPOSED TO BE A GREAT DAY!

I was expecting a quick pass through security, which I have enjoyed for three decades of travelling by air. But this morning our security lane came to a screeching halt. Some of the bags in our lane were held under the scanner longer than usual, apparently for a more detailed evaluation.

I was thinking, "Well, maybe they can't make out an iPad, or the telephone wall chargers, or the car chargers, or the iPhones, or other electronic gadgets that now control our lives and that we take with us on our trips."

The TSA agent motioned to an Atlanta airport police officer who then walked over to the security scanner. The officer looked at the scanner screen with a frown. He stared at a black leather briefcase bag that had just exited the X-ray scanner and asked loudly, "Who does this bag belong to?" No one in the area confirmed that it was his or her bag. I began to think it might be mine since I was waiting for my bag to come out onto the conveyor belt.

But then it hit me like a brick wall. I glanced over at the scanner monitor and saw a pitched black outline silhouette of a handgun. In fact, it was a Colt Mustang 380 semiautomatic pistol that I inherited from my father in 2001 when he passed away.

"OMG, I left the fucking gun in the bag!" I thought with angst.

Anxiously closing my eyes in uncertainty, I let the officer know, as he looked around cautiously, that it was my bag by raising my hand like a first grader volunteering to answer a question in class. He picked my bag up off the conveyor belt and walked up to me and asked, "Do you know why we have your bag?" Since I had just seen the gun silhouette on the screen, I disappointingly said, "Yes, I do."

The week prior I made an "around the world" road trip to several cities in Florida with my wife and son. I had placed the pistol in the glove box of the car, which I normally do on road trips for added protection in case the car broke down on a dark empty road. One of the hotels where we had stayed during the week had only valet service to park the car. With valet I didn't want to leave this gun in the car, so I threw it in my black leather work bag.

And then forgot all about it.

As a career executive with a national publicly traded medical real estate company, I have enjoyed a very good life. This great life is the result of a good family, extensive hard work, significant sacrifice, and lots of risks, planning, and saving. On this day I was working out of my home office, as I have done for several years, earning good money, and I was headed to the airport in the late morning.

This July day was extra special, though, because my travel schedule included no business meetings, hospital C-suite presentations, or market research. It wasn't filled with client meetings, cold calls, or conference calls. This particular trip was simply a low-key, "employee appreciation" event to bc held in Chicago, sponsored by the company. My employer at the time, based in Chicago, had invited select executives from around the country to fly to the Windy City for the sole purpose of enjoying an employee gathering with wonderful food, drinks, and a perfect outfield venue to watch a Chicago Cubs baseball game at Wrigley Field. While there for the night, we were to stay in the finest Chicago hotels with spectacular views and superb drinks and appetizers. I even received an official Chicago Cub's baseball cap via FedEx from my company a week before to make sure all attending employees were set, ahead of time, for the amazing night that was in store.

It was a beautiful day in Atlanta. I awoke to a cool summer morning, kissed my wife of 30 years good morning, and told my 13-year-old son good-bye as he headed out to summer football practice. And we have two other successful grown children who live in their own homes. What a great way to start the day.

The morning was off to a great start. It included coffee, breakfast, a shave, a shower, the good mornings, the goodbyes, and the rise and shine. I specifically arranged for a later departure from the Atlanta airport so that I wouldn't be inconvenienced with an early morning high traffic commute to catch the plane.

My flight was scheduled for 11:30 am from Atlanta to Chicago. And I was not even bothered when the electronic departure panels later indicated that the flight was delayed until 12:20 pm; because this was going to be a very relaxing and enjoyable morning and afternoon, with a nice flight, a short stint at the corporate office, and then a fun-filled evening with colleagues from around the country at the Cubs baseball game with food and drinks on three party levels at the amazing venue in Chicago.

I packed lightly with one change of clothes. And, since I "go commando," I don't need to pack underwear. I also packed some hairspray to keep my limited hair from "poofing" out like Bozo the Clown, and I packed a shaving kit and some deodorant. That was it. And I always take my black business bag. My bag is like a house-call physician's work bag. Everything personal is in my "black bag," including prescriptions, aspirin, Rolaids, hand lotion, hand sterilizer, my laptop, iPad, pens, markers, measuring scales, and business notebooks. Even my flash drives, business cards, candy, electronic chargers, and chords are in my bag. I always take the black bag onto the plane instead of checking it because I keep it in my personal possession at all times.

I decided to check a separate travel bag, though; because I wanted to take the larger hairspray can, which was the best hairspray that keeps my hair under control. The larger hairspray cans cannot be carried on the plane because of the size limit at the security checkpoint. Also, I like aerosol deodorant versus the rub on type, which to me feels greasy. I had the full-size spray deodorant can, which you also can't take on the plane.

I have flown since 1983, so I know the carry-on rules of flying. Nothing over 3.4 oz, no water, no clippers, no knives, no guns, no aerosol spray cans. The only thing I take through security is my black business bag, with all my "goodies" in there. I was ready to go.

In preparing for my trip, I checked and double-checked everything, yet I felt as if I was missing something. To make sure I had everything covered, I verified that my umbrella, my Chicago Cubs ball cap, business cards, prescriptions, pens, and iPad were in the bag.

On the hour-long drive from the far northern suburbs to the Atlanta airport, because I left later in the morning, I missed all the crazy traffic, brake lights, and stalls. Usually the radio traffic report is the same report every morning. The helicopter reporter states, like a daily recording, "I-285 is blocked; Hwy 400 is stalled; Spaghetti junction is backed up for miles; I-20 has brake lights all across the city ….." Even though I missed the traffic, all the way down, I still felt as if I left something back and forgot something for my trip; or something just didn't feel right.

The question was what?

I parked my car in the Hartsfield Jackson Airport remote parking. The bus was prompt and picked me up right at the car and I was dropped off at my terminal entrance with no hiccups at all. I quickly proceeded into the terminal to check in.

At the check-in kiosk all went well. I had an assigned seat, but the plane was noted as being delayed from 11:30 am to 12:20 pm. I didn't think the delay was too bad considering this was to be an amazing fun filled trip and not a traditional business trip. I felt lucky that the plane was departing out of the T-Gates, which are the closest gates to the north security checkpoint at the Atlanta airport. I had no lengthy walking or trams to ride. I had no escalators to take and no moving sidewalks to endure. I only had a brief walk through security and I am right at the T-11 gate, which was actually in view of the security checkpoint lane.

I am even a long-term "pre-check" flyer with TSA. This means that I am a credentialed flyer, a preferred flyer, or an executive flyer. I was a flyer that is pre-checked and is "so trusted" that he doesn't have to remove his coat or shoes, or even his electronics out of his business bag. This morning I can see my gate ahead, just past security, and looking forward to a couple wonderful days in Chicago.

The police officer asked the group of travelers waiting for their bags to get through airport security, "Whose bag is this?" as he was holding it up like a trophy after a sports star winning a championship.

It hit me then why I felt, earlier that morning, that I was missing or forgetting something as I left for the airport. I realized at that moment, feeling like a dipshit, that I had left my gun in the black bag.

After confirming to the officer that the bag he was holding was indeed my bag, he asked me to step aside to an open square workstation with four-foot high plastic laminate walls, next to the T-Gates security. The police officer and my bag were inside the cubicle, and I was on the outside leaning on a stand-up countertop. No one asked me another question after that moment, except one officer asked, "You forgot it was in there, didn't you?"

"Yes, I did," I answered, thinking that this would be no big deal. I told the officer that I have read about these people, including celebrities and NFL coaches that forget that a gun was in their bags at airports. And I have always wondered how in the world can anyone forget a gun is in their carryon bag? I have often thought that you must be pretty ignorant to not know that a loaded handgun is in a bag, especially while going through an airport. And here I am, forgetting that a loaded gun was in MY bag at the airport.

All I could think to myself was, "Wow! Holy Shit! I can't Fucking believe I did this, you moron."

The officers politely escorted me along the entire length of the airport terminal, likely the distance of four football fields, into a very small on-site police precinct located in one far corner of the airport terminal. The precinct is located inside the main terminal, past the ticketing counters, and beyond the baggage claim areas. During the walk, not a word was said. I assumed I would be questioned and given a ticket or fine of some kind.

I just didn't know what would happen next.

ARRESTED?

I am inside a police department for the first time in my entire 53 years of age, except for the time in grade school when we took a field trip to a jail in my hometown, Memphis, Tennessee. I recalled that day of the field trip when the policeman locked us kids in a jail cell with bars on it.

I thought at that time, "Man, I never, ever want to be in a jail as long as I live." It was dark and gloomy, and creepy and scary. The police officers during the field trip kept telling us, "You kids better act right and always do the right thing because you never want to be here."

After the airport policemen asked me to take off my suit jacket, they took me to a small area behind an extended wall, and there they frisked me. I was told to place my hands on the wall, spread my legs, which allowed them to grope me all over. I swore to myself that I was going to now have the infamous cavity search where they search all the orifices on your body for anything that might be hidden "out of view."

Fortunately, the search did not advance to a cavity search, but they emptied all my pockets to gather my Chapstick, which my siblings and I have been addicted to all our lives, and my orange fiber cloth that I use to clean my progressive lens glasses several times a day. They took at least three antacid tablets out of my pant pockets. Since my college days I have kept several antacid tablets in my pockets in case of an emergency heartburn or nausea event coming on out of the blue. They took my keys, my cell phone, and my coveted work bag. They took my belt, apparently in case I wanted to end it all by hanging myself in the little airport jail cell they were about to place me into.

I have, since my high school days, felt that I looked thinner with a belt on. And when I wear dress slacks without a belt, I think I look chubbier. Plus, it just isn't cool. I mean dress slacks with no belt? Just a shirt tucked into beltless suit pants looks goofy.

At least I knew I was being placed into the small cell alone, so I had some comfort knowing that no one would be able to see me in the goofy looking beltless slacks. I was finally placed in the tiny cell.

The cell at Hartsfield Airport is a room about five feet wide by maybe nine feet deep. The space is completely barren except a built-in wooden bench that is located along the back wall, across the five-foot dimension. I sat on the bench facing a door with a two foot x two foot clear glass window in the upper half.

It struck me, then, that I actually had just been arrested! I never felt arrested prior to that because the police officers didn't tell me I was being arrested. The police did not read me my Myranda rights. And they didn't question me as to why I was carrying a loaded gun through an airport. Nor did they ask me to where I was flying. I was surprised they didn't ask if I was headed to Yemen, Tehran, or the beach, or to Chicago to mingle with coworkers across the country, to wine and dine, and attend a Chicago Cubs baseball game; and to be wearing the brand-new official Cubs hat that is wedged in my work bag, sitting on the officers desk, out of view of my little window on my cell door. It was very surprising that no one asked me anything at all. I was just sitting in the 5 x 9 cell with the built-in wooden bench.

I was compelled after a few minutes to knock on the window and ask the officer, "Uh, excuse me, but am I being arrested?" The officer said, "Yes, we are booking you here, and we will then be transporting you to the Clayton County Jail."

I thought, "The Clayton County Jail? Holy shit!"

When watching the nightly Atlanta news, Clayton County is where the majority of the murders, rapes, robberies, car-jackings, and most other hardcore criminal activity occur. Clayton County is located in the southeast area of metro Atlanta and shares the massive Atlanta airport property with Fulton County. The way Atlanta airport security is structured, I learned, is the Atlanta Police Department, or APD, covers the actual airport facility and airport property. And Clayton County has jurisdiction for housing the criminals, jail, and court proceedings for any arrests made at the airport. So, in this crazy unexpected scenario, I am arrested by the APD, but will be transported to the Clayton County Jail.

I am stunned with, "WOW!" "OMG!" "FML!"

THE AIRPORT CELL

I asked for my cell phone so that I could make a call. The officer provided me the phone to make a call or two and told me that they needed the phone back. My first call to anyone in the world was to my wife. I can say confidently that she never, ever answers her cell phone, but today she did answer, and man was I glad that she answered.

All I could say, in a very calm but deep voice was, "Hey Wanda, you know that gun we moved from the glove box to my black bag at the valet when we took the Florida road trip last week?"

"Yes," she said.

"Well, it is still in my work bag," I replied. I continued, "And I am at the airport sitting in a jail cell. We need to get an attorney immediately!"

I made it clear to her that I had been arrested

and they are transporting my ass down to the Clayton County Jail. I told her that Clayton County is where most of the murders, car-jackings, rapes, robberies, and many other types of violent crimes occur. I told her that Clayton County is located southeast of Atlanta, at least one hour from our home in far northern suburban Atlanta.

I told her, "I am not spending the night in the jail, and please get me out ASAP!"

It took a while for her to believe me. She thought I was kidding because I never really act serious. She said, "No, you are not arrested."

"YES, I AM, Wanda! I am sitting in a friggin jail cell at the airport!" I said quietly but sternly.

Once I convinced her that this was really happening, she had a very good idea to call one of our neighbors, who was an attorney. Our neighbor quickly recommended a referral to another attorney with a high level of experience in Clayton County.

The wheels are now in motion by my wife to get the right attorney engaged, advise our two older children, inform other key family members like my brother who lives in the Atlanta area as well, and a couple of close friends of mine. Since I couldn't keep my phone long, I had to rely on Wanda to get all of this moving. I told her I loved her, and I would try to call her later. The police wanted the phone back.

After a very long time, I am still in the small dark

cell located at the airport where I sat, and sat, and sat, for what seemed like an eternity. I am wondering what's going on. I am placed in the cell at 10:30 am, and here it was 12:30 pm. There were no questions. There were no explanations or instructions. There were no people in sight. I am just sitting on the bench.

In my boredom while staring at the floor, a small single ant caught my eye. He is walking on the floor at full speed, seemingly scouting out the "territory." He was a tiny black ant that looked like just a small moving speck. I watched him as he moved closer and closer to my shoe while he walked at high speed and in a zigzag route. He would walk two feet to the left, then one and a half feet to the right. Then he moved one and a half feet to the left and then two feet to the right. I wondered if he could smell my presence since he was approaching me. I wondered if he could sense my shoe within a reasonable distance.

I wondered how or why did this solo ant get into the APD precinct in one far corner of the Atlanta airport nowhere near an exterior door or window to the outside. I felt that this little ant has a life just like I do. He is doing his thing, just like I am. He is making a life, just as I have. Even though he was in the same jail cell as I was, he was free, and I was locked up, and I was pissed, but still amazed watching him. I watched him making his zigzag route left, right, forward, and then backwards. And I watched him for another hour.

While the first ant wandered all over the concrete floor of the cell, a second ant caught my eye. The second ant was also small and black, making a rapid zigzag path on the other side of the jail cell.

I wondered if the two ants knew each other and were scoping out the same cell. I wondered if they were going to meet up at some point in their separate crooked routes. I wondered if they knew or felt like they were also locked up in the jail cell like me.

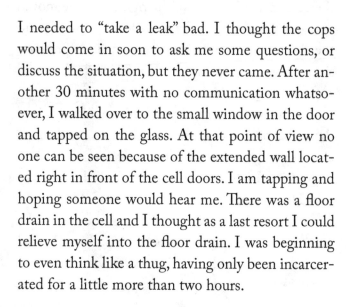

I needed to "take a leak" bad. I thought the cops would come in soon to ask me some questions, or discuss the situation, but they never came. After another 30 minutes with no communication whatsoever, I walked over to the small window in the door and tapped on the glass. At that point of view no one can be seen because of the extended wall located right in front of the cell doors. I am tapping and hoping someone would hear me. There was a floor drain in the cell and I thought as a last resort I could relieve myself into the floor drain. I was beginning to even think like a thug, having only been incarcerated for a little more than two hours.

Luckily an officer came to the door and yelled through the glass window, "Yeah?"

I told him, "I need to pee like a racehorse!"

He said, "You can go to the restroom, but I will have to go with you."

"OK, that's fine," I replied.

He opened the cell door and I proceeded to walk out of the cell and he put his hand up to stop me to say, "Now, I have to tell you this. You are free to head upstairs to the rest room. I will be accompanying you, but if you try anything, I will definitely taze you. And we are tazed in training, and believe me, you don't want to be tazed."

I said, "I am not going to do anything, and no I don't want to be tazed. I just want to take a leak."

We made a joint trip to the "John." He stood about two feet behind me as I peed in the urinal. I kept a look out with my left eye to make sure he wasn't going to taze me unexpectedly. But everything was fine, I zipped up, and he escorted me down the open staircase and back to the cell.

I sat for another long hour or so.

In the cell, I was allowed to use my cell phone again to follow up on some of my previous calls to my wife, kids, and close friends. I had received a tearful voice mail from my 13-year-old son, who said, "Dad, sniff, sniff, I hope you get out man, sniff, sniff! I love you, man."

That was tough, but fortunately I was able to send him a text to say that I was going to be fine and would be out in a few hours. During this time with my phone, I was able to verify that my wife had secured an attorney for $3,500. The attorney advised her that I would probably be spending the entire day and night in jail.

I thought, "Damn, this is really happening."

For some period of time while sitting on the wooden bench, I had that strange feeling like, "Is this a dream, or is it actually happening?" I simply could not believe that I was headed to jail for the first time in my entire life.

I have always abided by the rules. I have never harmed anyone.

I have never stolen a single thing. But, I am headed to jail. Not just ANY jail but, of all jails, the Clayton County, Georgia Jail.

THE DRIVE TO CLAYTON COUNTY

At nearly 1:30 pm, the APD officer came to my cell and said he and his partner are transporting me to the Clayton County Jail. I was asked to step out of the tiny room, past the extended screen wall, and into the open office space of the airport APD precinct. There the two officers gave me my gun-less bag, my phone, my Chapstick, my belt, my little orange eyeglass cloth, and asked me to put my suit jacket back on.

I felt at that point that I was good to go, until one of the policemen asked the other, "Do you want to wait until we get to the jail to cuff him or do you want to cuff him here?" After a brief hesitance, the taller officer said, "No, let's go ahead and cuff him now."

They asked me to turn around, and they cuffed my arms behind my back. This is the first time in my life I had ever been in handcuffs. They were much tighter than I had imagined, with very little room to move even my wrists. In order to get the cuffs on, I had to remove my watch. Once handcuffed, one officer carried my work bag and the other grabbed my right elbow and we proceeded to walk out of the APD airport precinct office area. We walked into the open check-in areas of the airport, and out to the main entrance past hundreds of people. Then they escorted me to a standing police car parked next to the passenger drop off curb.

I felt as if I was in a scene from the national news covering a mafia or politician arrest. I am in a black suit, with handcuffs behind my back, while holding my head down, being escorted through the public areas by two police officers and thrown into the back of a police car. As they do in the movies, the offi-cer holding my elbow helped me into the car, while stating, "Watch your head." Then they tossed my bag over my knees to the left-hand side of me sitting on the rear seat of the car.

I was surprised to learn that the rear seat was a non-cushioned hard plastic bench seat, similar to a seat on a theme park ride like a roller coaster. I also noted that there was very little knee space, if any at all, obviously to restrict body movement for the arrestee. The car is designed specifically to make one under arrest to be as uncomfortable as possible with very little wiggle room. The tightly cuffed hands were now at my lower back, pressed against the hard plastic seat. And with no knee space, I was forced to spread my legs at a nearly 180-degree angle to prevent even more pressure on my hands behind my back.

It was raining heavily on the police car ride to the Clayton County Jail. One officer was driving, and the other officer was in the front passenger seat. As we drove out of the airport property and onto the interstate loop making our way to I-75 south, I listened to the policemen discuss complaints about various procedures, other cases, other arrests, the driver's girl-friend, and many other irrelevant topics of my arrest. To me the only thing that mattered was where I was going, and that was the Clayton County Jail, the county notorious for the hard-core crimes in the Atlanta metropolitan area. I still could not believe where I was headed and couldn't believe I was sitting in the back of a police car with my hands cuffed behind my back and my legs spread as far as possible, like a damn frog.

During this unfamiliar drive, I was able to

consciously take note of the street names, landmarks, signage, and buildings. I felt as if I were kidnapped and was being taken to a hideaway place. And I wanted to take note of where I was going in case I needed to provide to authorities some type of information as to where I may have been taken. I made sure to remind myself constantly to keep a level head and to not freak out. I learned long ago that a level head helps keep the mind clear, prevents panic, and allows for logical solutions to be thought through. So that is what I decided I was going to do.

When we arrived at the jail, there was a large covered drop off area, similar to a large Vegas casino drop off canopy, but without the dazzling lights. This was just a very large dull brown canopy. I thought that there must be a lot of arrestees that need to be accommodated by that sized canopy. It did come in handy, however, because on this very rainy day, we were kept dry while exiting the police car and approaching the entrance to the jail.

The officers opened the back door of the car and asked me to step out. I was expecting them to help me out of the car, like they always do in the movies, which is the only place I had ever seen a man in tight handcuffs having to get out of the back seat of a car. However, as it turned out, they didn't help at all. It is interestingly difficult to squirm out of the hard plastic seat, with little or no knee space, with handcuffs wrapped tightly on your hands behind your back and lifting yourself half sideways from a seated position to a standing position while your legs are spread like a frog.

I noticed that the cuffs got tighter on the drive over, because the pressure of my back against the hard plastic seat helped to push the cuffs tighter. After I rose out of the car, both officers escorted me inside, holding both of my elbows tightly. One of them carried my work bag inside for me.

THE INTAKE PROCESS

Once inside the county jail, the very first thing that they did was search me, remove items from my pockets, and frisk me. Unlike the airport police, the jail staff here put on some blue gloves, while telling me they are about to search me. Since they placed blue gloves on, similar to the gloves worn by my proctologist, I knew for sure that the cavity search was coming. They started with removing my handcuffs, which was actually quite nice. The handcuffs hurt because of their shape and were extremely tight while your arms are pulled behind your back.

As soon as the handcuffs were removed, my suit coat was removed. All pockets on my jacket were searched and there they found my boarding pass for the plane trip to Chicago for the wonderful night I was going to enjoy hanging with colleagues from around the country, eating, drinking, and attending a Chicago Cubs baseball game.

They also found a pen. I have always been a pen fanatic, desiring unique pens with nice ink, different styles, and unlike all the 20-pack gel pens for $4.99 at the office supply store. This pen was an India ink permanent marker, with a 1.0 weight, that creates a nice, crisp, clean, bold line when I write or draw. Even though in today's electronic world, I tend to take notes and write on an iPad, it is always good to keep a real ink pen in your pocket for those emergency moments when you really need to write something down the old-fashioned way.

In my right-side pocket of the sports coat, they also found four antacid tablets, two ibuprofen, and one Allopurinol pill, for my Gout condition. These pills were a cause for a closer look. The jail staffer who was searching me looked as if he was hoping that he found some illegal drugs, pills, or contraband as he put the pills right up to his face for a closer inspection. Then he walked over to a brighter light and looked at the pills longer and more intently. I thought that he was feeling that he got some free "loot."

Luckily, he realized these pills and tablets were not important and he tossed them into a small steel trashcan nearby. He then took my coveted Chapstick, and my little orange cloth that I use to clean my progressive lens eyeglasses. That was it.

As he pulled my pockets inside out to the outside of my pants, he told me to keep the pockets hanging out, so that he could remember which inmates he has already checked and who he had not yet searched. He proceeded to pull up and out the front left pocket, the front right pocket, then the back left pocket and the back right pocket, and all were dangling completely out of my pants. I felt that this has got to look pretty goofy. I mean standing there with all four suit pant pockets pulled out and dangling outside of the clothing. But then I reminded myself that I am now in a fortified jail, in Clayton County, Georgia, and realized who the hell cares what you look like!

Lastly, he asked me to take off my belt, socks, and shoes and to stand against the wall. As he approached me with the blue plastic gloves, with me facing the wall, I got that uneasy feeling of the upcoming cavity search. I cringed.

Luckily again, he only checked me thoroughly for any objects that shouldn't be on me when entering a jail. After that he tossed me some Crock slip on shoes. I learned later that if the incoming arrestee has black socks on, he must remove them and is given Crocks. If the arrestee has on white socks, he leaves those on and he is given flip flop sandals, with the one thong for the big toe.

It looked funny later to see these grown men

with white socks on while wearing sandals with the toe slot crammed between the big toe into the white sock. From a jail perspective, I really appreciated having crocks because I was now sock-less with crocks on, rather than having a thong forced between my big toe and second toe, while wearing thick white socks. In retrospect, maybe the crocks were for the white-collar inmate, with no prior record, so that his time in jail is more suited to his lifestyle. But, I doubted it.

The next "station" along the probably 50-foot-long intake counter is where the jailers go through your belongings to take note of what you had with you upon entry. This is very important so that when and if you are released, you confirm what items you leave the jail with matches the items you actually came in with. But here, they kept my Chapstick. I asked if I could have one last lip application and the lady behind the counter told me no.

And that was my first worry. I thought, "How in the hell can I get by with no friggin Chapstick?" I have had Chapstick with me since my high school days, or over 30 years. And the lady wouldn't let me keep my little orange rag to wipe my glasses, or my Gout pills to treat Gout. I am now worried about having a painful Gout attack while in jail, and not have the emergency medication to treat it.

My other real concern is, "How can I get by with no Rolaids for that unexpected hit of acid indigestion?"

After going through my bag, my wallet, my keys, my credit cards, my Hilton Honors card, and other awards cards, all my airline club cards, my business cards, my files, and various papers, parking receipts, etc., everything was documented on a sheet of paper, then signed by me to verify what was being taken from me prior to my first time in jail.

As I was about to sign the form, I noticed there was no iPad! I asked the lady behind the counter, "What happened to my iPad?"

She said, "What iPad?"

I was amazed at my assertiveness while being arrested. I looked her in the eyes and said, "There was an iPad in that bag when I walked in here, and now it's not there."

She opened the bag and tilted it towards me, and said, "See, there was no iPad."

I then yelled down to my left, towards my first stop on this long intake counter, and told them very sternly, "There was an iPad in this bag and now it isn't here, so someone took it."

They mumbled amongst themselves at the first station and told me they never saw an iPad. I told the lady at my station that someone took the iPad. Not that that got me anywhere, but I at least wanted her to know that I knew the iPad was missing. I told myself I would have to deal with it later. I know that Apple has a way to locate lost or stolen items, and that's what I intended to do as soon as I got out of the slammer.

After confirming my items, except for the iPad, I was asked to walk into the next station that was a small one-room medical clinic, which was generally a standard medical examination room. The clinic was just a single room full of cabinets, a sink, an office desk and a side chair. The elderly nurse, with crooked teeth, messy hair, scratchy voice, and lots of freckles asked if I had ever had a Tuberculosis shot. I told her I probably have, but not exactly sure if, or when. Since I was not sure, she felt the need to give me a TB shot to determine if I had been exposed to TB. This was quick and simple and I was told to watch the shot location for any odd reaction over the next few days. Due to the anxiety of being in jail, I never really remembered to check the spot location for any reaction during my stay, but apparently everything was fine.

The nurse had a great sense of humor. I am rarely

serious and act silly most of the time. Surprisingly, I was able to also act up in jail too and I had her laughing in no time at all. I liked her because her weighing scale weighed me 10 pounds lighter than my 20-year-old scale my wife keeps under her vanity in the bathroom of our master bedroom in north Georgia. I told her that I really liked her scale. She swore it was accurate, but I know it is 10 pounds too light. I didn't want to push it because she uses that scale on herself, so I am sure she feels great knowing her scale is accurate to the tee.

In the clinic we reviewed any known allergies, conditions, and illnesses. I told her that I had Gout, and that I really wanted to keep my Gout pills, just in case I needed it, due to some unexpected flare up. No one wants to live through a Gout attack if you can help it. I have lived through several Gout attacks since 1998, and some were very severe. I swore then that I would keep my Gout pills on my body at all times, just in case, because you never know in advance when you may have a flare up.

I was very disappointed when she said that they couldn't allow that. She explained that "if" I had a Gout attack, I would have to get the clinic-supplied Gout medication at that time. She assured me that the jail does stock some Gout medication.

But my real disappointment came when the nurse told me I could not keep the Chapstick. I told her I don't see how in the world I could convert a Chapstick tube into a weapon or use the tube of Chapstick as a suicide tool after they took my belt. She roared with laughter through her scratchy, crooked toothed grin.

I was asked to go back to the long check-in counter to sign some final intake paperwork. This lady behind the counter, for some reason, needed to know the color of all of my clothing. And I do mean ALL my clothes. I am standing right against the counter. The counter is 30" tall at sit down height for the lady and then there is glass from 30" up to about six feet high. That day I was wearing a black suit with a tan short sleeve dress shirt with no tie and a white tee shirt under the dress shirt.

"What color yo shirt?" asked the lady.

I am standing there right in front of her, and I looked at my shirt, then looked back at her with a strange face and said, "Tan!"

The lady was writing down my answers to her questions on a separate form. "What color yo pants?" she asked.

I said, "Black."

"What color yo socks?"

I said, "They were black, but now I don't have any on because they took them from me."

"What color yo tee shirt?" she asked.

I said, "White."

Then she asked me, "What color yo draws?"

I asked, "My 'draws'?"

She said, "Yeah, you know, yo draws?"

I then realized she was asking about my underwear, underpants, or my under "drawers." Well, back in the early 1990s, I started noticing when I wore underwear it really bothered my left testicle. I dealt with it for years and years and years. I went to several medical specialists including the urologist, surgeon, and internists, and no physician could find anything wrong with me. And then it occurred to me that apparently the undies were just too tight or causing some kind of compaction under my regular pants. I tried briefs, and boxers, and other styles of underwear. Nothing seemed to help, so I tried not wearing any "draws" for a while and actually loved it. Beyond the freedom you feel, the testicular pain was gone immediately. So, commando was the new way for me.

Again, she asked me, "What color yo draws?"

I said quietly to her, leaning to the voice hole in the glass, "Commando."

And she looked at me with a strange face and asked, "Commando? Is that like flesh color?"

I said, "Not really flesh color."

Then she asked, "Well, what color is commando?"

And I leaned over to the glass again and whispered, "I ain't got no draws on! So just put down clear as the color."

And she looked at me with big white eyes and a strange face and said, "Oh lordee, lordee, you got clear draws on?"

With a fear of this fact getting out in the jail, that the only man in this 400-person jail is running around with no draws on, no telling what might happen, so I stressed to her, "Don't you dare tell this to a soul, and I mean no one!" I feel she actually did tell this to somebody because later on I was given a jumpsuit that was three sizes too big and split on the side from my chest to my knee. I had to walk around gripping the side of my jumpsuit to keep it closed so no one would see that I was commando.

As I continued checking in, I told the counter staff that I needed to use the restroom and she said, "Head in there," while pointing to a room with a large window in the interior wall and a door with a half window. I walked in, thinking there was a bathroom inside of this room. As the door closed, I immediately realized that I was in a locked holding pen when I saw a brushed aluminum toilet unit in the corner of the room. The toilet was just placed in the wide-open room. There were no screening walls and no doors to the toilet area. There was a small built-in sink where the toilet tank would normally be on a residential toilet.

In the room were also two big black men, one standing and leaning against the window, and the other sitting on a brushed aluminum built-in bench that wrapped around 3/4 of the wall space in this 10' x 15' room. I get stage freight when I pee alone in my own bathroom, much less having to take a piss in front of other people. But in this jail I told myself, I cannot appear at all to be quiet, shy, or bashful, because that could be a sign of weakness in this roughhouse jail in Clayton County, Georgia. So, I confidently walked up to the toilet, unzipped my fly, and peed like a racehorse! And what a relief it was.

When I was finished relieving myself, I went back up to the door to go back to the counter to finish the check-in activities, and I learned that the door was locked from the outside. That is when I realized, "Man, I am actually literally getting locked up!" I tapped on the window in the door with my knuckle to get the girl's attention at the counter, but she ignored me. Then I waved to the funny nurse who walked by, who I had laughing and who

I thought would be my friend, but she just walked past me.

I realized again, "Damn, I am actually locked up and these people don't really care that I want to get out of this open-roomed pee hole, with two scary men inside, that are probably in for murder."

With nothing else to do, and no one "on the outside" giving me any attention, I wanted to directly address these guys in the same locked up room that I am in.

I started by saying, "Man, this place is a joke." They both looked at me and nodded in agreement. I asked them what they were in for. I assume that's the way you ask a fellow inmate why they were there. I wasn't sure if you ask, "Pardon me, sir, but I was just curious why you are here with me?" Or would you ask, "Why the hell are you here?"

But what kept coming back to me is probably what comes to mind for every inmate. I've seen it on TV a thousand times. "What are you in for," just came out naturally to me, with ease. And the guys must have heard that before too, because they were very anxious to answer that question. The bigger man sitting on the bench told me he was in for a probation violation for a drug offense. And the other man said he was in for a misdemeanor drug offense. I immediately felt more at ease than before, since they were not "in" for murder, or robbery, or rape. I figured if it was just a drug offense, they wouldn't be raping me or killing me in jail. I wondered if they saw my inner relief at all. I was hoping they didn't.

Obviously, the next question was from each of them. They wanted to know what I was in for. They, like me, using my line, asked, "What you in fo?" I was again assured that this phrase must be the standard universal question from one new inmate to another, because I saw it on TV and now, I heard it in reality. When they asked me, I told them I was in for taking a gun through security at the airport. And they both surprisingly gasped!

They looked at each other and ironically; they seemed to be the ones that were a little nervous, being in jail in the same room as me, the lone white guy.

They asked me, "So you are in for a gun violation?"

I said, "Yep."

They were in with the guy with a gun offense. We didn't have much more time to "chat" because the lady at the counter came and got me out of this open pee room. I was a happy guy at that particular moment.

At the counter I was asked to sign more paperwork that documented my personal articles that I had in my possession when checking in to the jail, and I had to acknowledge my arrest charge. The charge was "possession of a weapon in an unauthorized location." This was the first time I knew why I was being arrested. I was also asked to sign a form that indicated that my time to see the judge was the NEXT day at 1:30 pm!

I knew, then, for sure that I was going to be staying overnight in the Clayton County Jail. I thought, "Damnit." I wanted to quote my granny who used to say, when she was mad, "Damnit to hell!"

GETTING ACCLIMATED

After completing the paperwork, I was asked to sit in what looked like a small doctor's office waiting room. Except it was open to the rest of a large open space that was probably 80' x 80' with low height modular walls with workstations and human heads sticking up above the walls. The staff was moving around, and it was odd seeing just the heads shifting from here to there. The small seating area had about 30 seats, with a bank of five pay phones along one of the walls.

I immediately walked over to one of the pay phones to call my wife on her cell phone. The phone charges were $15 per minute and the person receiving the call must accept the charges. She, again, luckily answered her phone. Honestly this was the second time she actually answered the phone since

1998 when we first got a cell phone. But I was happy. I told her that they are telling me I cannot go before the judge until 1:30 PM, tomorrow! I told her that I did not want to spend the night in the Clayton County Jail, period. She told me that she got with the attorney, and he also said my court appearance is at 1:30 the next day, and that yes, I am spending at least one night in jail, if not longer. A sinking feeling began to encompass me.

I asked her to figure out the damn amount of the bail, any cash required, do they accept checks, credit cards, etc.; whatever it takes. I asked her to check with the attorney to see if I can pay more money to get out tonight instead of tomorrow. I asked her to do whatever it takes to get me the hell out of here! I told her I loved her and goodbye, and then I sat down in one of the "doctor's office" chairs.

Not in a planned way, but as new inmates congregated into the waiting area, all the African American men were sitting on one side, and I, the lone white, was sitting on the other side. It reminded me of high school dances, or youthful wedding receptions, when all the guys were on one side of the room and all the girls on the other side of the room. But in this case it was about a dozen black men on one side and one white man on the other.

A guard walked by. He had no gun, or weapon, but he talked and acted as if he did.

He said sternly, "Hey, everyone get a seat on the back wall!"

He yelled again, "I said everyone get a seat on the back wall!"

I was already sitting against the back wall. When the other new inmates shifted to the back wall, this forced a younger nice looking man to sit right next to me. He was cool, smooth, had a thick beard, and a good smile.

A couple minutes later he asked me the infamous, "What you in fo?"

I am thinking, "My god, I am in the hood, in the jail, and people are actually asking me what I am in for."

I just couldn't believe I got myself into this crazy situation. I was thinking how stupid it was of me to "forget" that a friggin gun is in my work bag as I traipse through security at the airport more than ten years after 911.

"I mean, come on, you stupid ass!" I thought. I reminded myself, I need to be stern, not wimpy. I thought if I acted strong and confident that I would at least convey the message that people may not want to bother me in this particular jail.

I told him that I was in for taking a pistol through the Atlanta airport. He also kind of "flinched" like the two inmates who were in the first open-air potty room I went in during the check in process.

He asked, "Damn! You took a gun to the airport?"

I told him, "Yep. That's what I did."

He went on to say he was in for testing positive on a cocaine test after a traffic stop. He told me he finally had landed a great job, making $29 an hour as an electrician, which equates to about $60,000 a year. He was very upset because he felt he could be working tonight rather than sitting in jail. He told me over and over that he could be working, making $29 bucks an hour but he is sitting in jail. I am sitting right next to him wondering why in the world would he be screwing around with cocaine when he has a family and a nice job.

For some reason I felt the urge to give advice. I told him that if he stays out of trouble, due to an increasing shortage in tradesmen, his career as an electrician should prove to be an extremely nice field for the long term. I told him how many tradesmen's children opted not to follow in their fathers' footsteps and instead focused on college to pursue law, medicine, or business.

I said, "The younger generation has pursued anything but an electrician, or painter, or plumber career. In today's economy a good electrician is hard to come by and therefore salaries are rising. In addition, in the future you have something you can easily do for yourself as a self-employed electrician."

I was stunned by the fact that he was actually listening to me intently. He really seemed to hear what I had said. I wondered then, if some of the people sitting in these jails have ever had anyone give them any realistic advice. I wondered if they have ever been in a situation to know anybody who might provide encouragement or direction.

Within a couple more minutes, I heard a loud demanding voice yelling my name. And then, again he yelled my name. I looked around and didn't see anybody immediately. He yelled louder. I stood up and could see over the dozens of low cubicle walls, across the big "inmate intake" room that a large white young guard was waving me over. I walked around the end of the sea of cubicles to the opposite side of the large space from where I was sitting in the "doctor's office" chairs. When I reached the other side of the room there was a huge black man, probably about 29 years old, 6'4" and about 290 pounds with discolored lips with white and pink blotches. He had a very deep voice.

He grabbed my fingers and began the finger printing process. This was actually a lengthy process. I wondered if my prints from the third grade at Knight Road school in Memphis, Tennessee are still in the system or not.

I asked, "Aren't my prints from Memphis in the system?"

He asked, "When they done?"

I told him, "They were done when I was in the third grade."

He chuckled and said, "No, they not in the system."

I was thinking that was odd. I have often wondered during my life if I ever left my prints on something during some type of crime, could they find out it was me? And I always thought about the third grade prints I had made in Memphis, and thought, well they do have those prints, so I better not leave my prints on anything. Now, after all those years I find out that I could have left my prints all over the country for the last 45 years because they didn't keep up with the prints that were made in 1971 in Memphis.

We proceeded with the finger printing process. He grabbed each finger individually, pressed the outer third of the finger, rubbed it on an ink pad, and pressed each finger on the paper, rotating it in such a way that the entire print from the far left across the bottom to the far right, is printed. If it were geometry, it would in essence be a 180-degree print of the under and side of each finger. So eight fingers later, and two thumbs, we were done, at least for now.

Immediately following this printing effort, in the same area, it was time for the infamous mug shot. I was told to stand with my back against a concrete block wall, look directly into the camera ... and "click." Then I was told to turn 90 degrees to the left ... "click," then turn 180 degrees to the right ... "click." I was thinking about all the celebrity mug shots, like Mel Gibson or Nick Nolte or the drunken politician. I was somewhat happy that my mug shot would look nothing like those because I wasn't drunk out of my mind or drugged up, but I now had an official mug shot.

I realized now why some inmates had what looked like an identification band around their wrist, like what you might wear while admitted to a hospital. The mug shot, and all personal information like name, height, weight, hair color, and eye color are printed on this band and then they placed the band on my left wrist. I looked at it and noticed immediately that the wristband noted the color of my hair was gray. And I thought, "What the hell, my hair may have a little gray in it, but I would not have described it as gray." I thought, "If I decided to break loose and escape from jail, they would be looking for a gray-haired man, not a balding black-haired man with some gray, so there is a chance I may not be recaptured." After the wristband was placed onto my wrist, I was taken to the other side of this small work area where they do more ink printing.

Here the large white guard told me we needed to make palm prints. I was thinking "Palm prints? They have definitely advanced quite a bit since my grade school experience in 1971." The guard got a little hand-held roller that looked like a small paintbrush roller, which added more ink to a 12 x 18 inch flat inkpad. And then he grabbed my hand and had me press my hand flat on the inkpad, then flat on the paper. After that he wanted me to press the right side of my right hand and the left side of my left hand flat on the inkpad, in a way that he described as a karate chop. Then he pressed the side of each hand on the paper. So now we have full prints of all rotated fingers, karate chopped hands, and palms of hands. I was waiting for the footprints like at birth, but they never requested these.

After all the printing, which turned out, indeed, like a major "process," I was told to go to room H11. There were 12 rooms numbered H1 through H12, similar to the open pee room at the initial check in area, but these were on the other side of the large open room with all the cubicles. They were lined up one after the other, H1 all the way to H12. I was walking towards H11.

H11

When I first entered H11, I was one of four inmates. One of the other inmates was a young black
man who looked about 15 years old, but I assumed
he was a bit older. He had a white sleeveless tank top
shirt on, with long blue jean shorts that went past
the knee, and he was wearing very nice tennis shoes.
He was on a bench across from me to the left. To
the left of him was another open-air stainless-steel
toilet, with the little round sink on what would be a
tank on a residential toilet.

Directly in front of me across the room sitting
on the bench was another black man who was likely
in his early thirties. He had neatly prepared rows in
his hair with short dreadlocks and a full beard that
was very short and clean cut. I was impressed by his
very nice clothing. He wore a nice Chaps checkered

green long sleeve shirt but slightly cuffed up on the wrists. He wore nice cut-off blue jean shorts and really cool tennis shoes. His name was Reggie, or as I called him, the Talker.

To the right of me on the same bench I was sitting on was another black man about 25-26 years old who was lying curled up in the corner, with a short-sleeved white tee shirt, black shorts, and very nice tennis shoes. He had his arms tucked inside the tee shirt as if he was cold. To me the room didn't feel cold, but I learned later that my cellmates thought it was cold in not only the room H11, but also the entire jail facility.

In this room we sat, and we sat, and we sat. The guards never told us any next steps, expectations, or instructions of any kind. We were just sitting in this locked room with a brushed aluminum bench wrapping the room, with an open-air toilet. We sat for hours.

The "Talker," Reggie, was talking, and he was talking, and he was talking. He told a story about his "WB," or Woman Bitch, using his term. "WB" is the reference that all of my inmate friends used to describe their "woman," girlfriend, wife, or partner. Reggie said his WB threw his stuff out in the woods. He described that this "stuff" included his other nice clothes, his pictures of his deceased family, his CDs, his possessions like radios, books, chess sets, and just about everything he owned. But in Atlanta summer of 2013, it was raining. Through August 2013, the total rain significantly surpassed an average full year of rain. It rained every other day, inches at a time, every week for months, it seemed. So, when all of Reggie's possessions were thrown into the woods behind his place, they were getting rained on and ruined. Reggie was totally pissed.

He said he went inside the house and took his WB's stuff and threw her clothes, CDs, and books all over the road in front of his house. He went a step further and took her car keys and threw them on the roof of a nearby gas station so she could not get to them.

That angered his WB so much they got into a physical altercation, including punching each other. And his WB called the police. Reggie and his WB both went before the judge and the judge not only locked up Reggie, but he also ordered that his WB be locked up too. So, Reggie and his WB are locked up at the same time, in the same jail. This story hysterically cracked me up. I tried not to laugh, but I did.

The Talker, though, went immediately into another story and then another story, and then another story. Reggie told one story after the other for hours in holding cell H11.

One of his stories involved his "prior WB," as he referred to her. He said, as he was pacing the floor of the room we were in, "Man she was beautiful, you know. I mean she was smart, attractive, sweet, smelled good, and looked good." He went on to say, "But man she was nasty!" Reggie relayed that one evening, he wanted to cook a nice meal for his WB. And he had romantic music and soft lit candles and good home-made food that he prepared himself. During dinner, his WB had to go to the bathroom. When she came back to the dinner table all was fine. Reggie and his WB were having a nice meal and a nice discussion, until he had to also go to the bathroom.

Reggie said, "I went to the bathroom, and I see on the toilet seat that there is all this black "shit" all over the seat. And I am like, what the hell is this shit?" He said he looked at it, got some toilet paper and rubbed it. He didn't know what it was. He said it wasn't literally shit, but he said, "It was some 'nasty black shit' that came off her ass onto my toilet seat!"

He relayed to us that he is a fine gentleman and cares about his women. He wanted to let her know that she is leaving some kind of black shit all over his toilet seat, so that she knows what's going on and it won't happen to her again at someone else's house. He said he truly cares about her. So he goes back to the dinner table and tells her, "Man, you nasty, man.

You WB is leaving all kind of nasty black shit on my toilet seat!"

After that she was pissed. He said she was offended, and she never got over it, and from that point forward he didn't want to be with her anymore. He told us in the room, "Ya know what I'm sayin? I mean I can't do no fucking that shit! That's nasty man."

We all died laughing at this story. The younger kid laughed, the young man with his arms tucked in his tee shirt laughed, and I laughed, and Reggie laughed. It was friggin hilarious. Reggie was telling this story while pacing the room, wailing his arms, and talking smack about his WB. OMG, it was so funny. I laughed my ass off.

After that story, Reggie slowed down a bit, and all of us in the room were just sitting there quietly. I was on the bench with my head leaning back against the concrete wall with my eyes closed, thinking, "What the hell am I doing in this rat hole?" And I wondered, "What the hell did I do? I have to get out of here."

As I was dozing off, I hear a voice ask, "What's yo name?" I ignored it, thinking this was being asked of someone else in the room. But again I heard, "Hey, what's yo name?" I then opened my eyes and saw that the Talker across from me in the room was looking straight at me.

I told him my name, or my fake name, that I for whatever reason wanted to use, was Dominic. Then the universal inmate question came. "What you in fo?" asked Reggie. I told him I got caught with a gun at the airport. As before when I mentioned this in the inmate check in area, all eyes in the room looked at me quickly. In this room H11, everyone impressively stared at me with their eyes wide opened, very surprisingly.

After another silent period, Reggie asked me if I had a license to carry a gun, and I told him, "No, I didn't have a license." Then he asked if I had a gun permit, and I said, "No, I didn't have a gun permit." Reggie didn't know this but in Georgia there is only one license, a Georgia Weapons Carry License. I did get a license after this ordeal, but it would not have helped my charge of weapons in an unauthorized location.

Then I leaned my head back again on the wall with my eyes closed.

As I tried to doze off again, Reggie asked me, "Hey, Dominic, since you have illegal guns, can you get me some guns?"

And I thought, "OK, here I am, never in jail in my entire life, I've never done anything illegal in my life, and I am sitting in the Clayton County Jail, now being asked by my fellow inmate if I can help with some illegal gun deals." I can either say, "Well no, I can't get any damn guns, are you crazy?" But, for some reason, I wanted to project to these experienced inmates that I am not all sweet and innocent. I concluded this was the best approach for personal safety while spending at least one night in the Clayton County Jail, while going commando. But in reality, I do have a relative who can get me some guns.

I told Reggie, "Sure I can get you some guns."

He excitedly said, "Really, man? You can get me some guns?"

"Yeah, I can get you some guns," just trying to fit in. I wanted to pick a place far away from Atlanta and told him I have a "cousin in my hometown," just randomly tossing out a person and a city far away from Atlanta, so that I wouldn't be expected to ever take him to actually get guns locally, should he ever find a way to contact me after we are released.

He said, "Where, is that?"

I figured if I threw out Memphis, my real hometown, that would end the discussion because it is a seven-hour drive from Atlanta. So, I told him I had a cousin in Memphis that can get some guns. But as soon as I said Memphis, Reggie yelled, very excitedly, "NO WAY, MAN. You from Memphis!?"

With a sinking feeling I told him, "Yes, I am from Memphis."

He immediately jumped up off the bench and rolled his long sleeves on the green checkered Chaps shirt up to his biceps to show me from his wrist to his bicep on his left arm was the word "M E M P H I S" tattooed in capital letters in the equivalent of a 120 size font, about two inches tall. And on the other arm, was the word "T E N N E S S E E," in the same huge font tattooed from his right wrist up to his right bicep.

And I thought, "Holy shit. I purposely try and toss out a town 500 miles from Atlanta, and he happens to be from that same town? Are you kidding me?" He now wants to know more about my gun-dealing cousin in Memphis. I had to start embellishing my story a bit from that point forward so that I didn't reveal any true identities, but only street names.

To my surprise, this Talker, Reggie, stood in the middle of the room H11, while pacing the floor, and told the entire group which had, by then, grown to more than seven inmates, while pointing to me, "Hey, ya'll, this dude is from Memphis man!" I am thinking, "Good God. Holy Shit."

He went on to say to the group, "Memphis is crazy, man. They cut you up over just a fucking cigarette," and he asked for my confirmation of that, when he asked me, "Don't they, Dominic?"

As a continuing way to blend in, I, of course, said, "Oh hell yeah, man. In Memphis you will be diced up just for a dollar! You don't want to mess with anybody from Memphis!"

Again, many in the room cringed as if that was hard-core or even gross. But suddenly I realized that I was getting a reputation of an illegal gun toting crazy dude from Memphis where they cut you up for nothing.

Right then, at that precise moment, of all things, the electrician man who I met while I was checking in, who learned of my gun incident, walked into the H11 holding cell. He immediately said, "Hey man, there is the pistol dude," while pointing to me. And the rest of the room, who had then grown to about 12 inmates all looked at me respectfully. I started to feel more comfortable as this "bad" reputation began to emerge for me in jail. Inside, though, I was laughing my ass off.

The story of what I was "in" for was now being told to fellow inmates by fellow inmates. The other inmates were told that I was the dude that was picked up for possession of an illegal gun at the airport, or that I was from Memphis, one of the most notoriously crime-ridden cities in the country. Again, all big wide opened white eyes were upon me.

I tried to act totally nonchalant about it as if this whole thing was second nature to me. And I felt an inner feeling of gaining "clout" in jail, which is what I had hoped would happen. But on the inside, I was also thinking, "I hope to hell I am not in here for two weeks. I hope to hell I am not beat up or raped tonight. I hope to hell I don't lose my high paying job. I hope to hell this is not in the newspapers tomorrow."

As the room filled up with inmate after inmate, I started asking my new roommates why they were picked up and arrested. I learned that nearly every person in room H11 was picked up for either drug possession or probation violation for a past drug arrest. And I was thinking, if this is typical of this entire jail, the impact of time, cost, taxes, money, life disruption, and family disruption that these drug arrests and probation violations are actually causing is flabbergasting. Most of the guys in this room were not violent people, most just had some misdemeanor drug issues.

Once again, after more humorous stories from Reggie, and a few more inmates were deposited into the H11 holding cell, things quieted down a bit, with no talking, no stories, and no laughter. We were tired.

I again, while sitting on the stainless-steel bench, trying to zone out, was wondering how long I will be in the jail, and what will happen next.

ONE IMPORTANT LESSON

I was sitting upright on the bench with my eyes closed, listening to some quiet discussion. I overheard Reggie, who was probably 34 years old, speaking to a very young inmate, who looked about 15 years old, but was probably at least 18 years old. Surprisingly, Reggie was advising the kid to not go down the same path he had chosen. He told him that it is a dead-end street, and it gets you nowhere. Reggie was encouraging the younger man to do better than he himself had done. Reggie then asked the younger man, "Why do you guys pay $10,000 for wheels for your car?" He told them that is an example of what was not a good thing to be doing.

But the younger man began to say that he came from nothing. He has nothing and never has had anything. He said that black people never have anything and are all poor. So, when he gets some money, he said, "I have to go get me something!"

I am not a very assertive person and I avoid all confrontations when possible. But in the Clayton County Jail, and I am the only white inmate in a sea of inner-city black men, I convinced myself that I HAD to blend in; that I HAD to participate in some way; and not sit quietly in the corner looking afraid of my situation or of the environment I was in. When I heard the young man say, in essence, that he has to spend $10,000 for wheels because the black man comes from nothing, and therefore HAS to get something when he gets his hands on any money, I decided to reveal a story about my father-in-law.

I told all the men in holding cell H11, now crowded with about 15 men, the story of my father-in-law. Some had just white tee shirts, some with white tank tops or under shirts, most with drooping-off-the-ass shorts; and Reggie with his polo shirt, and nice jeans.

I opened my eyes, raised my head off the concrete block wall and said, "Wait a minute!" Instantly, I had 30 wide-open white eyeballs staring at me, as if, "OMG, he hath spoketh!"

No one uttered a word, and the room waited for my next words. I continued to tell them, "My father-in-law was raised in a shack. He had less than any of you guys have."

I told them, "My father-in-law had no money growing up, and I mean zero money. His house had a dirt floor. His house had no plumbing. The electricity was limited to a single bulb hung in the middle of the ceiling in a big room, from an extension cord that ran from outside the house."

I told them, "I guarantee you that everyone in this room has significantly more than that right now."

I said, "He was so poor that he only went through the 6th grade, he picked cotton, and he worked the fields. And at 14 years old he moved out of his house and went to Memphis, Tennessee, from a dirt poor town in north Mississippi."

All the men in the room were staring at me intently as if they never knew that there was such a thing as a poor white man, or that there was such a thing as a white man who had picked cotton as a child.

I went on to tell them, "My father-in-law, after moving to Memphis, began painting houses, and went on to be one of the most successful house painting contractors in Memphis, ultimately being hired by Museums and CEOs to paint the largest mansions in town."

I told them, "Because of his extreme poverty as a child, instead of buying $10,000 wheels with the first money he earned, and because he never wanted to be poor again, he invested ALL of his extra money. He invested in stocks, bonds, mutual funds, and utility stocks. He has had a financial adviser for 40 years and now has a very nice nest egg and portfolio."

I told them that because of his poverty, he would NEVER blow $10,000 on wheels. And I ended it by suggesting to my cellmates that in lieu of blowing their money, that they should look to invest it like my father-in-law did. It could change their entire life.

The room was silent.

Even though I was finished with my story, all eyes were still trained on me, and not one word was spoken. I wasn't sure if they resented that my father-in-law was now just another well to do white man, or that they felt that what they do with their money is none of my business. In jail, I thought to myself, "I am not quite sure what would set off another inmate to jump me and pound my head into the stainless-steel toilet bowl." No one really said a word about my story. All my cellmates eventually looked other ways, settled down into their comfortable positions to wait out the holding time in cell H11.

During the few hours that I was in this same holding cell, I looked over to the toilet several times, hoping I would not be forced to take a crap in the toilet in front of 15 cell mates. This was one of my fears throughout my stay. But I did have to take another leak. As I did before in the intake cell when I was with the first two inmates who I thought were murderers, I knew I had to act nonchalant, with confidence, and walk up there to the corner of this crowed room and unzip my fly and take a wiz.

So I did. And I did so with a very high level of confidence!

TIME TO EAT

During my third hour sitting on the bench in the same cell H11, the guard suddenly came to the door. He slightly opened the door and began tossing our dinner in, which we had to catch with our hands. The dinner consisted of two slices of wheat bread with two thin slices of bologna wrapped in clear plastic wrap. He also tossed us a Styrofoam six-ounce cup, and a package of dry powdered water flavoring. The water was to be retrieved from the water dispenser and sink located and built into the stainless-steel toilet tank.

As we all waited to fill our cups with water, Reggie yelled out to all of us in the room, "Don't put the powder in the water!" He again yelled, "Don't put the powder in the water!"

Someone yelled back at him, "Why not?"

He told us that the powder contains a sterilizer that is used to keep the sexual urges down for men in jail. He said that way rapes and masturbation are reduced drastically. He swore that this was the case and has been the case for years. Several other men quickly agreed with him. One man said that after his last stay in the Clayton County Jail, that he could not "get it up" for a month!

As I was laughing hysterically inside, I also wondered if this was true. If true, I hoped that every inmate in the room with me would mix the powder with the water. One of my concerns with being in jail was the chance of being raped in prison, especially with me being commando.

I began encouraging all of them to go ahead and use the powder by first using it myself and telling them that this can't be true. After I mixed my lime powder with the "toilet" water, one or two cellmates followed my action. But most others only drank the plain water. I was hoping for more men to mix in the "sterilizer," because it might get out that I was in the jail with no "draws" on. But most of the other men didn't mix the powder in the water. My only option, then, was to just hope that I was not jumped later that night.

THE JUMPSUIT

Shortly after the "tasty" dinner and sterilization water, a different guard came to the holding cell. He told us it was time to change into our official cell clothing. I wasn't expecting to have to change clothes for a one-night stay.

I thought, "Damn, I am commando, and now I have to disrobe. I hope it will be set up to change in private instead of changing together in a large group. The last thing I needed to reveal is that I am commando, with a bunch of Clayton County inmates who didn't consume the "sterilization powder."

The guard asked us to all step out of the holding cell H11. He relayed the instructions for disrobing and changing into an orange jumpsuit with "Clayton County Jail" stamped across the back of it. We were all given an orange jump suit and a clear plastic bag about the size of a lawn bag or large kitchen bag. We were told that when we are changing, to place our pants, shirt, and under shirt in the bag. We were told to keep our under drawers, or 'draws', on.

Again, I thought, "Damn, they will now know for sure that I don't have any 'draws' on. Shit!"

We were told to place our paperwork with our name on it on the bottom of the bag, and then add our clothes on top of the paper, then tie a knot in the bag. This way they will know who the clothes belong to when checking out of jail upon our release.

We were taken as a group around the corner where all the showers were located. I thought, again, "OK, here we go. Its cavity search time! Damnit!"

I was surprised that the showers were six to eight individual showers or at least showers that are divided with a little side wall. I was expecting the showers to be built like an open gang shower you might see in my high school back in the 1970's. We were asked individually to step into a shower stall and change into the orange jump suit. We were also told that a guard will be watching us while changing to make sure we were not hiding anything.

I finally was asked to step into a stall. I placed my paperwork on the bottom of the bag. I placed my

T-shirt in the bag. I placed my dress shirt in the bag. I was moving very slowly hoping the guard would leave for a second before I removed my pants. He never left, so I slowly removed my dress pants and placed the pants in the bag.

While standing there completely naked, I was going to quickly get into the jump suit, but the guard asked me where my "draws" were. I embarrassingly told him that I was commando that day. He asked me to turn around with my back to him, and to bend over. Again, I swear to God, I braced for the cavity search as I was bent over in front of a 6'4" well-built security guard at the Clayton County Jail, while standing in a private shower stall.

I was thinking, "What the fucking hell am I doing in here. How stupid ass of me to take a friggin' gun to the Atlanta airport. I want to be home with my 13-year old son, playing basketball, or cooking dinner with my wife of 30 years, or speaking to either of my grown son or daughter on the phone, or enjoying a wonderful company gathering in the outfield at a Chicago Cubs baseball game, with free drinks and first class dinner with colleagues from around the country. But 'NNNOOOOOOOO ', I am standing butt naked in a private shower stall bent over forward grabbing my feet, with a huge handsome well-built guard behind me, bracing for a cavity search."

I am thinking, "OK, here we go! Let's just go ahead and get this over with!" as I quenched my face in anxiety.

After a few seconds of bending over forward, to my extreme relief, the guard told me to go ahead and put my jumpsuit on. I am certain that he saw the big smile on my face, which was an expression of relief and happiness that the cavity search didn't happen. Although he may have had other conclusions on why I was smiling after bending over naked in front of him, I was just happy to be placing clothes on again.

It was a bright orange jumpsuit that was at least four sizes too big for me. The legs dragged the ground, and the arms fell 2-3 inches past my hands. I felt like I was wearing a Memphis Tent and Awning fabric with a fly hole in it. I am six feet tall and weigh about 220 pounds. Why I got the jumpsuit for Andre the Giant, or the Hulk, or a 6'8," 350 pound man, I will never know. But at that point I also didn't care. I had to roll up my sleeves and roll up my legs so that I could walk properly.

One unusual detail that was noticed immediately was a large rip on the side of the jumpsuit. This rip was in the seam of the right side of the jumpsuit, and it was about 18 inches long running from just above my right hip, to about the middle of my right thigh. I realized that my rape fears were not gone.

While commando, one doesn't want to be showing his skin from his upper hip to his knee around prison. I thought, again, "DAMNIT!"

H12

After our group of inmates had changed into the jumpsuits, we were taken into another holding cell. This room was labelled "H12," which was very similar to H11. It was a concrete block walled room about 12 feet by 14 feet in size. The door was solid steel except for a small square window on the upper portion that was about two feet x two feet. This cell however did not have a built-in stainless-steel bench or open toilet like the check in bathroom room or the H11 holding cell had. We all stood against the wall or gathered on the floor along the perimeter of the room.

As before in H11, Reggie began telling his funny short stories and small talk was held amongst the inmates in separate discussions. And I was, again, just trying to zone out to convince myself I was not really in this place. But I was, and I was pissed.

After a short period of time and Reggie's storytelling, everyone started to relax and not talk so much. There was a lengthy dull period of dead silence in this holding cell. We were tired, bored, and uncomfortable. All 20 of us by then, just sat. We were all on the floor because this room had no bench. Our eyes were closed or half open. We glanced at each other occasionally. Some stared out of the little window in the door, as if they too were wondering why they were in this place. Others slept in the corner, curled up in a ball.

Suddenly, in the midst of such a solemn moment, the electrician started to sing. He was singing a song from a television show. This was a vibrant song, but one that I was not too familiar with.

The song was happy. The lyrics were joyful. The beat was celebratory.

As the electrician sang louder and louder, and with more emotion and movement, the Talker decided to pipe in too. I was in my obscenely oversized orange jumpsuit that was split down the side, sitting on the floor of H12 in the notorious Clayton County Jail; the only white man in the room of 20 men; listening to a couple inmates singing a song.

It was indeed a stunning display of sheer talent. This was something you would see on America's Got Talent, or The Voice, or even a live concert. The act promoted happiness, togetherness, and enjoyment. I just sat on the floor of the cell, with my back against the wall, looking up at the two standing men, and listening. I listened as these men belted out one of the best versions of a duet I have ever heard! It was absolutely incredibly amazing.

All the other inmates just watched and listened as I was doing, all staring at these two entertainers. This continued for about 15 to 20 minutes. When they were complete with their act, you couldn't help but clap, as you would at any concert or show. I am now clapping at two fellow inmates for an unbelievable song rendition, in jail, while holding my ripped jumpsuit together to hide my commando situation. It was really enjoyable, amazing and fun.

I thought, "It beats sitting at home playing pool on my iPad, or checkers on my home computer." I admitted to myself, though, that it isn't better than a first-class evening with free drinks and hors d'oeuvres in the outfield party venue building at the Chicago Cubs baseball game, mingling with company colleagues. I was still pissed that I was stuck in this jail, but it was entertaining, nonetheless.

Following the songs, there was another long span of complete silence. Now into the fourth hour of sitting around the jail intake holding rooms, the members of my group, including me, were tired, trying to sleep and basically just hanging around in total quiet.

In the midst of the silence, one of the inmates who hadn't said a word all night started to speak. He was one of the few fellow inmates who had good looks, was well groomed, and very sharp. He was a tall thin man nearly 35 years old with a close shaven goatee and moustache. Once he began speaking it was clear he was also very educated and very articulate.

His story centered around his recent trip to Africa, the "homeland," as he called it. All the other inmates, who were all African American, were very intrigued that this inmate had been to Africa. He described his visit to an area on the western coast of the continent. The placed he referenced was the center point of the origins of the slave trade. This was where most of the global slaves were sold, separated from their families, boarded onto boats, and shipped to just about anywhere in the world where slavery was rampant. The other inmates asked specific questions of him, like what was the room like at the harbour, or describe the dock, or what did he learn, or what did he see.

I decided to not say a single word during this discussion, because as a white American, I knew that I couldn't relate to how a black man felt about slavery. And being in this room with all African American cellmates, I didn't want to cause any negative discussion amongst them about the era of slavery. I just listened.

The speaker described the stunning hills, the beautiful landscape, the panoramic sea, and the region as a whole. He described how amazing it was to see and how much history there was to learn. As I listened, he went on to state that he saw beautiful castles on the hills. He also toured these very large and opulent castles.

He told the group that the castles he toured were not owned by white men. He relayed that they were built and owned by black men. He told us that their own brothers lived in these castles, while selling their own people. He outlined that he now understands that white men were not the only drivers of slavery, nor was it just America, but the whole world and all races were involved in slavery. Even some Africans themselves profited greatly and became very wealthy through the slave trade.

The other inmates were very surprised to hear him say this, and one young man asked him, "Are you saying black people sold black people?"

And another inmate asked him, "Our own people made money out of slavery?"

And he said, "Yes they did."

Again, I chose not to say a word during this discussion because I WAS the only white man in the room.

After he relayed his story, there was another period of long silence. During which, I thought to myself, that I also didn't realize that the African blacks
profited off slavery, and I was just as surprised as my
cellmates. I felt some sense of relief for some reason
of my being the only white man there. I felt that
this storyteller, by default, removed some of the re-
sentment that some of the cellmates may have had,
indirectly, towards me for American slavery.

MOVING ON

After another hour or so, the same guard came to the door and asked us to all step out of the H12 holding cell. While in this group, he said he would be taking us to our overnight cell areas. He emphasized during this walk to follow these very strict rules,

"Don't speak a single word!"

"Always face forward!"

"Stay in a single file line!"

"If a female inmate or a female officer is in the hallway, do not dare to look at her. You will turn around immediately and face the wall, until I say clear."

"Is that clear?!"

We all complied, "Yes sir!"

After leaving H12 and the intake portion of the building, with the check in, waiting area, holding cells, and changing areas, we stepped out into a very long corridor probably 400 feet long and 12 feet wide. The corridor had no windows and was built with concrete block walls. In a single file line, we walked slowly along this long stretch of nothingness. The lights were very dim and not a word was spoken. Just a long quiet single filed walk.

Once we arrived at the end of the hallway, we all made a left-hand turn and stopped. I heard the clanking of automatic door locks and squeaking doors, as a large set of double solid steel doors opened fully, allowing us to walk into another section of the facility.

We entered into a very large area that looked like a gymnasium. This area had one basketball goal and floor to ceiling exterior windows covering a two-story high wall. This was in one small corner of an even larger open space. The larger section included a control station in the very middle. This control station was manned with two or three guards in a "fish bowl" glass enclosed work area. From this control station every one of five large cellblock enclosure suites was visible. Each of the cellblocks included nine cells on the first level and nine cells on the upper level with a staircase coming down the left side into an open area with red built in steel tables and chairs for eating.

Rather than going directly into the cell areas, we

were taken into a classroom on the first floor of the gymnasium-like area. This classroom was not unlike a traditional high school or college classroom. There were about 25 seats in the room. The seats were individual seats but fixed to a row of about eight seats each. The back of the room was all glass overlooking the large gym-like area. The front of the room had a long eight-foot plastic foldout table. And on two sides of the room from the floor to about four feet high, were stacks of large plastic buckets. Each bucket was about two feet wide x three feet long and about two feet deep. I wasn't sure what was in the buckets. No one was at the front of the room. Our group just sat there in a seat waiting for someone to show up to provide us further instructions.

This was another long wait, probably about 30 minutes. In this room the seats were at least cushioned and covered with blue vinyl. They were more comfortable than a stainless-steel bench or sitting on the floor itself as we experienced in the holding cells.

I didn't talk much in this room. I was getting the sinking feeling that this is the real fucking deal. I thought, "I was actually going to now be spending the night in this rat hole." I didn't feel like talking anymore. I was done. I wasn't interested in hearing Reggie's stories. I didn't want to listen to anyone singing a song. I didn't want to hear about $10,000 wheels, or drug offenses, or domestic violence. I wanted to get the hell out of there.

I was in the third row from the front of the room and most of the inmates were to the rear of the room, or behind me. While sitting, and sitting, and sitting, Reggie, behind me a few rows, started talking to the inmate sitting right beside him. He and the other guy began talking about cocaine. They spoke with specificity how to smoke crack and how to use various pipes and tools. They discussed how cocaine powder is split and separated with a razor blade. They spoke of how best to snort cocaine once it is separated. They spoke of the highs and the lows. And they spoke about the good and the bad.

They described in great detail how much better sex is while high on cocaine. They discussed how much money they spend with the various levels of dealers, and distributors, and street corner thugs who are selling it.

Reggie asked me then, "Yo, Dominic, are you getting all this?"

I ignored Reggie.

Then he and his seatmate began advising me that I should do cocaine. They were telling me that it was cool. And that it was great. But I was zoned out at that point. Not asleep but zoned out.

I wasn't responding.

I didn't care to add to the conversation.

I don't care about drugs.

I have never tried even marijuana or any other drug in my lifetime.

I had no interest getting into crack or cocaine discussions with the hood in the Clayton County Jail.

So, I just waited and waited, while Reggie and his colleague laughed and laughed and presented more and more graphic details on drugs, women, and "good" times, and drug induced sex, and high's.

I was thinking to myself, "This is really all that these guys do. All that is on their minds are drugs and women and sex. It's all they think about. It's their entire livelihood. It's their income source. It's crazy and it's a waste." I thought, "Why is it my problem to take care of these stupid asses when they do get caught, killed, or get into trouble. They have no goals, no ambitions, and no responsibility. They exist like wild, running around the streets. They emphasized mostly unbelievable details, about sex, drugs, and crime. That was all. There was no discussion about goals, ambition, their jobs, their houses, or their children, or their families." I was actually getting pissed having to listen to this bullshit!

Eventually another inmate, dressed in an all-white jumpsuit entered the room. I was told by one of the men in my group that the white jumpsuit represented a "working" inmate. They said these are the guys who have a few months instead of a few days to be incarcerated. With that much time in jail, they can earn time off or possible reductions if they agree to help do some work around the jail. This guy in white was the one who described our next activity.

He told us to each grab one of these big plastic tubs surrounding the classroom. When I grabbed my tub, in it was a rolled up sleeping mat, about one inch thick, 18 inches wide, and six feet long; a white sheet, a thin wool plaid blanket full of holes, a hand towel, about four inches x four inches for drying ourselves in the cell if we had to wash our face or hands, a Styrofoam cup for water, a cheap toothbrush, and a tiny tube of toothpaste. Once we had the tub, we exited the classroom and proceeded into the larger cellblock area.

THE CELL BLOCK

A tall, thin, well-built, good-looking guard escorted us to the first level gathering area of one of the cellblocks. The overall jail had a pretty nice design. The center control area, where the glass bowl was, is surrounded by five very large cell-holding units, each with a two-story glass wall facing the center control area. Each holding unit was set up in such a way that a large gathering area is on the first level immediately inside the entry door to the unit. In the gathering area, there were about six or eight three-foot-square steel tables with four individual steel built-in seats, one seat on each side of the table. The tables were red.

Along one wall on the left-hand side of the first level was a bank of silver pay phones, designed like what one might see in a 1980s airport. The gathering area was a two-story atrium-like space and there was an open staircase adjacent to the left-hand wall that went to the second level. The second level had nine individual cells with an open continuous balcony running along the front of the cells, with the door to the cells facing out into the atrium. The doors and the atrium are visible from the central "fish-bowl" control station. The lower level behind the eating area, and below the second-floor level, was a bank of another nine individual cells.

Also in the center of the atrium area were concrete block walls that were half-height, about four or five feet high. Behind one of the walls was a shower, and behind another wall was a toilet with a built-in sink. But there were no ceilings. With this design, from the second-floor balcony you could look down and see someone sitting on the toilet or taking a shower!

The guard was very, very strict and he said he was the one who will give us the rules while incarcerated. He said the rules were expected to be followed by everyone. The guard advised that if the rules were not followed by the inmates, an additional day or two could be added to the time of incarceration. He began by describing what was in each of the plastic tubs that we each carried into the cellblock. He was to tell us how to make the bed. He said, "Any time you are out of the cell, the bed will be made! Is that clear? And it will be made exactly like Earl is going to show you!"

He motioned to a black inmate in a white suit, another worker inmate. Earl was about 55 years old, 5'8" tall, and heavyset. Earl took a mat from a tub and unrolled it flat on the ground. He proceeded to unfold a sheet and placed it on the mat. He pulled the sheet very tight across the surface of the mat as he tucked the flat sheet tightly around each corner. The sheet was wrinkle-free on the mat and tucked in very neatly at the corners. Earl then unfolded the thin wool blanket, which had worn holes in it, and stretched it out over the sheeted mat. The blanket was tucked under the mat only at the bottom and at the sides of the mat. On the head of the mat, the blanket was folded back about eighteen inches so that the sheet can be seen at the top part of the mat.

The guard asked, "OK, now is this clear? Are there any questions?"

"No, sir," we all said.

He continued, "We will check on your mat several times a day. If we see your bed is not made up exactly how Earl demonstrated, we will find you and make you do it the right way. And you DON'T want us to have to come find you. Is that clear!?"

"Yes sir!" we all replied.

After everyone felt comfortable with the bed-making rules, the guard explained that a cell has been assigned to each inmate. He outlined that each cell has two cots in it. And he was going to list which cell we are assigned to. I thought to myself, "I hope to hell I don't have anybody in the same cell as me. I don't even know how to act in jail, and I would rather just be by myself. And I don't want anybody messing with me in that cell. I don't want to get roughed up or even raped in there." I was thinking all this while tightly gripping my ripped-at-the-waist, drastically oversized jumpsuit.

MY CELL

Surprisingly my name was the first one called. The guard yelled, "Dominic, Cell 9, upper left." Cell 9 was at the immediate top of the stair. I was told to proceed to the cell with my tub, as he continued to call out the other inmates by name and their responding cell number. As I made my way up the open stair to the left, I heard familiar names being called out by the guard, "Willie, Cell 2. Reggie, Cell 6. Robert, Cell 7....," until all the inmates in my group had been called and assigned a cell.

I was exceptionally pleased that no one else had been assigned to my cell. I was ecstatic that I indeed had a cell all to myself. I was relieved with joy that I wouldn't have to worry about being bothered by anybody else locked up in the same cell with me. Even in my cell all alone, my mind was still blown.

I mean, here I was in a friggin' orange jump suit locked up in a jail cell in Clayton County, Georgia. I just could not believe this was happening!

The room had concrete block walls painted a dull tannish yellow. It was an approximately seven foot by twelve foot room with a two-inch thick solid steel door with a small window about three inches wide and 24 inches tall along the right side of the upper half of the door. In the room were two steel cots built onto the back wall, across the narrow dimension of seven feet with the same dull yellow paint. The first cot was mounted on the wall about 18 inches off the floor and the upper cot was mounted about five feet off the floor. Above the upper cot was a small translucent window running horizontally, about one foot tall and four feet wide. It only allowed minimal natural light in but had no exterior visibility. It was only there to provide indirect natural light into the cell, as if this was to make the inmates feel better emotionally based on some PhD psychological study. I can tell you that the window was a waste of money because no real light is coming into the room. Therefore, I really didn't notice it. And even if I did notice it, I still felt like crap because I was in jail.

On the right-hand side of the room there was a dull yellow painted steel shelf maybe five feet off the ground. The shelf was about four inches deep and 12 inches wide, with extremely sharp 90-degree corners that were open corners to the room. The shelf was just attached to the middle of the wall. But it was an extremely solid shelf. Under the shelf were four built in hooks, probably for the small hand towel that was included in the plastic tub because there was nothing else in the room that could be hung on a hook. We had no baseball caps or jackets, nor belts or bags. All we had was the little washrag.

In the corner of the room, to the immediate left of the cell door, was another of the same stainless-steel toilet and sink combination with no doors, walls, or screening. The sink is in the top of the toilet tank. I was thinking that this was a very efficient toilet design, accommodating all the plumbing in one tiny spot. Above the toilet-tank-sink combo was a mirror. The mirror wasn't a glass mirror but a shiny sheet of stainless-steel in which one can fairly reasonably see his reflection on the steel.

I caught myself wetting my hands and rubbing water through my very limited hair and trying to brush my hair with my hands, because we had no hairbrushes. My brother later told me that I was a dumbass, because nobody, he emphasized again, NOBODY, worries about their damn hair in jail! I had thin but nice slicked back watered-down hair that looked good. Our father always taught us to look presentable in public, so by God that's what I was going to try to do.

I laid the mat out on the bottom steel cot. I then unfolded, tucked and wrapped the sheet, and then folded and tucked in the blanket, exactly like the guard instructed. I was always one that went by the rules. And for some reason I wanted the best-looking cot in the jail. I made sure every single wrinkle was out of it and that the blanket was folded back exactly 18 inches. I considered calling the guard to come in and see it. I was proud of my mat.

The white towel was sized between a hand towel and a small washcloth. Its only intended use was to wash a face or dry some hands. I took it out, rinsed it in the sink, and washed my face. I squeezed it out and hung it on the hook below the shelf. I then claimed that hook as mine. I was astounded how I was claiming little things in this tiny cell. I claimed the bottom cot to be my cot. I claimed the hook on the far right to be my hook. And I was prepared to defend it should someone at some point try to steal my cot or my hook.

After washing my face, I looked around the room. There were no clear windows to look out, no books, no chairs, no tables, no TV, no computer, no iPad, and no cell phone. Nothing was in the room at all except me, the wall mounted cots, and the sink toilet combination. So, I just laid on the cot. Even though there was nothing to do but lay on the cot, pillows were not included in the plastic tub. There was not enough height between the bottom cot and the upper for me to sit on the cot, so laying down was the only option.

After about two minutes of laying on the mat with no pillow, I started to figure out how to develop my own pillow. I didn't want to use the blanket or the sheet because I didn't want to have to remake the entire bed constantly to keep the guard happy. And there was no clothing available like a T-shirt to be used as a makeshift pillow. The only possible item that could even come close to a pillow was the washrag. The rag was only slightly larger than a domestic regular washcloth. This one was about four inches x six inches in size. I got up off the cot and grabbed the wet towel from my hook. I folded it in half, then rolled it as tight as possible into a ball or almost a small cylindrical shape. It was like a mid-sized rock at that point, but it was a soft rock. I placed it right behind my right ear. I chose my right ear because when I sleep in my house or at a hotel or at a relative's house, I sleep with my face pointed towards the door. I do this just in case someone comes in the room at night. By facing the door, I can easily see who it is by opening my eyes, and if need be, I can jump to defense instantly. This little pillow amazingly provided the perfect height to keep my head from being totally flat on the mat. I realized quickly how easily you can make yourself proud. I was beaming with pride knowing how to makeshift a "pillow" in jail.

I laid down on the cot just looking around the cell and on the underside of the cot above me, dwelling on how the hell I got in here and when will I get out. Then I started thinking more like a hardened criminal.

I wondered what would I do "IF" someone got into my cell and wanted to do harm to me. I have never been a real fighter, but I have become, when faced with danger, what I call the Tasmanian Devil on occasion where I will become a totally different personality, like a crazed whack job. In high school, there was a situation when a classmate in the locker room jumped me out of the blue for no reason whatsoever, while I was sitting on the ground in front of my small locker after P.E. class. My natural instinct was to immediately get off the floor, which is a disadvantaged state by default. Then I instinctively rammed this guy's head into the lockers. I rammed his head into the metal lockers on the right side of the aisle; and then I rammed his head into the lockers on the left side of the aisle. I did this while cussing like a crazed psychotic lunatic. He cried in front of all the guys changing clothes, rubbed his head, and walked away.

By the time I made it back to my chemistry class, following the P.E. class period, I was now the guy, from my classmates' perspective, that "kicked Mark's ass." All the students in the room were asking me about it. I relayed that I didn't kick anybody's ass. But the story had spread quicker than I could downplay it and by the end of the school day I was suddenly known as a major fighter.

I learned basic self-defense while growing up with three brothers who would regularly jump me without warning, or I would jump one of them without warning. And the four of us would wrestle almost every day for hours. We taught ourselves various techniques to pin the other one down. My brothers and I could likely force our opponents to "tap-out" like in the UFC cage fighting rounds. When additional measures were needed, if we were faced with an opponent outside of the family, our weapons usually would include inanimate objects like lockers, door jams, or car hoods. Inanimate objects are harder than fists, cause more damage, and protect your hands.

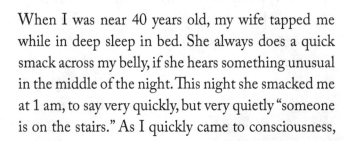

When I was near 40 years old, my wife tapped me while in deep sleep in bed. She always does a quick smack across my belly, if she hears something unusual in the middle of the night. This night she smacked me at 1 am, to say very quickly, but very quietly "someone is on the stairs." As I quickly came to consciousness, she said again, "someone is on the stairs." My strategy was to throw the intruder off guard by acting like a total crazed loony bin, or like a whacked-out nut job, by making unrecognizable noises and screams while flailing arms about while running full speed at the opponent. At least this gives you time, during the intruder's slight confusion and delay, to ram their head into a doorjamb, or, in this case, to kick them down the stairs. So that is exactly what I did.

I immediately jumped out of bed, acted like a total crazy loony bin, or like a whacked-out nut job, by making unrecognizable noises and screams while flailing arms about while running full speed at the opponent. I had planned during his slight confusion and delay, to ram his head into a doorjamb, or in this case to kick him down the stairs. Within one second of my planned ramming his head into a door jamb and kicking him down the stairs, I heard my 16-year-old son yell, "DAD, ITS ME, DAD ITS ME… WHAT ARE YOU DOING!?"

I can say it scared the hell out of him, and me, and my wife. My son acknowledged that there actually was a slight delay of confusion on his part while figuring out what was going on. So, in my mind this proved my defense theory works in a real situation.

My plan of defense in my jail cell was this. If someone came into this room to jump me, or to harm me, I would become the Tasmanian Devil instantly. I would scream and yell unrecognizably, arms flailing, and looking like a wacked out crazy loon. Then in the opponent's confusion I would ram his temple into the extremely hard 90-degree square exposed corner on the solid steel shelf hanging on the wall five feet above the ground. He would be confused, then down, and would never know what happened. I thought this through four or five times and had it planned perfectly. I only hoped no one would actually come into my cell and jump me, because, even though I am not a real fighter, my family can attest that I would actually do this as planned. I assumed if you are jumped in your own jail cell and have to defend yourself, you might not be charged, even with murder. But I didn't want to find out what would happen. I just wanted to get out of there.

But it struck me as odd that I was plotting a potential kill. This is something I had never done before, but I was surprised how naturally it felt while in the circumstances I was in. And I was convinced I would act on this deadly plan if the need arose.

As I laid there, at what I believed was near midnight, I was thinking about my job, my family, my career, my legal expenses, my bail, my father's gun that they took, my belongings taken, my missing iPad, my court date, and my wife. But I was full of joy that I had a cell to myself.

Somehow, I finally dozed off.

NEW ROOM MATES

Suddenly, without any notice, all the cell doors in the entire cell block area unlocked at once. All the lights in the jail came on, and the guard in the control center yelled into a loud speaker, "Everyone get up!"

It was very odd because I had no watch, or cell phone; nor iPad or laptop; nor TV or clock. So I had no idea what time it was. The tiny horizontal exterior window above the upper cot was so translucent it wasn't evident if it was light or dark outside. I doubted that this "window" was connected to the exterior. I felt it was more of a visual element only simulating a window and was not a true window.

As soon as I raised my head from my egg-shaped washrag pillow, and stood up, not one but two new inmates were coming into my cell. I told them,

"Hold on, I only have one extra cot!" They both just came right in anyway; walking right past me like this was just a normal event for them. They seemed to know exactly what to do as if they had been there many times.

One man was a tall, thin, extremely dark man. He was probably 30 years old, 6-foot tall and 140 pounds. He reminded me of Michael Jackson when Michael Jackson was black. He said in a very feminine voice, "I am just going straight to bed."

The other man was an older looking gentleman, who I thought was 75 years old, but learned later he was only 52, likely the result of a hard life. He had a grey beard and moustache and was balding. When he came into the cell, he said he was sleeping on the floor. Both men had their big plastic tub with their mat, washrag, sheet, and blanket inside. The thin man quickly unfolded and unrolled his mat and linens and jumped into the cot above mine. The older man made his mat on the floor and laid down.

It was late.

Being raised in the south, and in an Italian close-knit family environment, I had empathy for others as well as good manners. My natural instinct was to offer the "older" man on the floor the use of my cot, and I would sleep on the floor. Just as I was about to suggest this to the gentleman, I stopped myself.

I told myself, "Now wait a minute! I am not at the mall; I am in jail. Politeness may be a perceived sign of weakness, and I had already convinced myself that I would show no signs of weakness whatsoever while in jail." So, I just laid back down on my cot and allowed the older man to sleep on the floor.

He chose to set his cot up where his body was against one long wall of the cell. The mat was perpendicular to my cot and abutted where my head was positioned, and I was about 18" off the ground. He was on the floor with his feet towards my cot and his head towards the cell door. I noticed immediately his feet smelled like raw sewage. I couldn't switch my position because I have to face the door as I sleep, allowing me to be as ready as possible if someone ever breaks into our house and goes into the bedroom. And I have to lay on my right side because I experience a dull pain if I lay on my left side, as I have experienced for 20 years. I knew it was going to be a long stinky night in store.

He was given flip-flop thongs for shoes instead of crocs like I had. He had thick white socks, with the thong of the flip-flop crammed between his toes. He told me in the cell that night that these shoes really hurt his toes. I had asked him why he got flip-flops and I got crocs. He added that if you are not wearing white socks when you are checked into the jail, you have to turn in your socks. And since you are then barefoot, they give you crocs. If you have white socks on when you are checked in, you are told to keep the white socks on, and they give you the flip-flops. He asked me, upon my release, if I would trade shoes with him so his feet wouldn't hurt. I told him I would, and I meant it.

The lights were on but dim at 4 am in the morning. It was hard to sleep because I was in a room with two strange men, in jail, with my head on a balled-up hand towel, and people talking loudly outside the cell door in the open area. The older man on the floor asked the standard introduction jail question. He asked me what I was in for. And I told him that I took a gun to the airport by accident.

After a lengthy discussion about him being picked up at the airport for trespassing, and after talking about his daughter working in an office position in the Clayton County Jail, I was asked how long I have been with my "woman."

I told them, "I met my wife when we were 16 years old, in the summer of our junior year in high school. And we dated five years, then married while a junior in college." I told him that I waited until a junior in college to ensure that I could actually graduate from college. I was asked if she ever got on my nerves or disrespected me, and I said, "Absolutely!" I told them, "After 30 years of marriage, of course she would get on my nerves occasionally."

Then I was asked, "How many times have I had to hit my woman!"

I asked the older man, "Hit my woman?"

He asked, "Yeah, how many times, you know, have you had to hit her. You know, when she deserved it?"

I was thinking, "Dang, this guy is serious."

I replied by telling him, "Ever since we met in 1978, through five years of dating, and 30 years of marriage, I have never struck, hit, punched, or threatened to hit my wife."

The old man on the floor looked stunned. And the thin gay sounding man on the top cot leaned over the bedside and looked down at me, while I was looking up.

He asked. "You never hit yo woman?"

I said, "No."

The thin man asked again, "You never hit your woman? Hum."

He said, "All men hit their women."

I strongly told both men in my cell, "It takes a bigger man to NOT hit your lady."

I told them, "Yes, had I ever liked to have popped her, yes. But a weak man will actually do it and a stronger man will not do it."

Again, a look of surprise was on their faces, as if they had never heard of this before. I began suspecting that most of the guys in this jail had never heard of this and expected that all men hit their ladies, woman, wives, WB's, whatever. I again emphasized to them that a bigger man does not hit his "woman."

I asked the thin "gay" man who again reminded me of a pitched-black Michael Jackson, "What are you in for?" He relayed, like many others had done, that he was in for a drug offense. He told me that he thought it was a total joke. He is working, paying bills, doing what he is supposed to do. But one day he was speeding and was stopped going 10-15 miles over the posted speed limit. This was in another county more than 60 miles away. During that stop the police officer found that he had a warrant from 3-4 years earlier for not showing up for court in Clayton County for a minor drug offense. So he was arrested and brought all the way from Cherokee County, Georgia down to the Clayton County Jail.

When the inmates on the first floor of the large cellblock area started talking loudly, yelling, making a lot of noise and basically acting up, the thin man told his cellmates, "I am not one of those jail birds. This is crazy. I try to do what's right and I am not one of these guys that come and go out of here all the time." He said he wanted to get out as soon as possible and that he isn't comfortable there like all the other guys are.

His story reminded me that the vast majority of the inmates are in this jail for minor drug offenses. And this emphasized, in my mind, how much time, money, and energy is wasted on these minor offenses. The significant disruption of people's and families lives, cost of the courts and public defenders, facilities, healthcare, and construction, while expending hundreds of millions of tax dollars.

While speaking with other inmates earlier in the night in the holding cell H11, I was told how they felt the entire jail system is a racket. I trusted these men because I had no experience in this segment of society, and they each have had multiple experiences. I thought, "So they must know more about this than me, right?"

They relayed that the county jail is paid by the state for each man or man-day in the jail. For each incarceration, the jail earns money from the state. The incentive state-wide is for each county to maximize occupancy, to build more jails, and to keep them as full as possible.

Even though I wasn't sure if what I was told was true, it was beginning to make sense because most of the inmates were having to spend the night, or multiple nights in jail, until they could make bail. Many who were incarcerated could not make bail, so they just sat in jail sometimes for months until their court date arrived.

I was feeling that the "system" WAS actually working against these guys versus working FOR these guys.

BREAKFAST

I slept on my hand-rag-pillow and managed to sleep for another hour or two. Suddenly the guards came into the cell bank yelling loudly and banging, "OK, EVERYBODY UP. EVERYBODY GET UP, MAKE YOUR BED, STAND OUTSIDE OF YOUR CELL."

Then all the cell doors magically unlocked and slightly opened. We all stepped outside the cell and stood next to the door. My cellmates told me that the guards have to see every inmate from the main control booth outside of the large cell areas.

As we stood, seemingly like in a full salute in the military, the guard advised us that breakfast was on its way, and we needed to be ready to pick up a tray, find a seat, eat our meal, return the tray, and head back to our assigned cell.

After standing outside the cell door for about five minutes, another inmate brought the breakfast trays into the large open gathering area below. He looked like he was an inmate helper because he had on a white jump suit instead of the standard orange jump suit. This assumption was verified later when I asked a man in a white jumpsuit why he was in white. He told me his time to be in jail is over six months. And as another man in a white jumpsuit told me earlier, to gain a softer sentence or shortened time, the inmates can volunteer to help out with various simple jobs in the jail. The man in the white jumpsuit bringing in breakfast trays was working and helping with delivering the breakfast throughout the jail.

My cell is on the second floor to the far left of the open balcony upstairs. The staircase led right up to my cell door. To get to the other cells, after getting upstairs in front of my cell door, one would need to make a right-hand turn and walk down the long open balcony made of steel and overlooking the open eating area below.

The breakfast trays were stacked on top of each other, already filled with food. The trays were three to four inch thick light brown plastic with recessed bowls or sections to hold the different types of food. This way the trays can be full with food, and still be stacked on top of each other. About 12 trays were stacked on top of one another in two adjacent stacks, both stacks sitting on a flat pushcart. And the man in the white jump suit then pushed the cart of trays into our large open cell bank area. The guard was giving instructions for us to grab a tray and have a seat, then the next inmate would grab a tray and have a seat.

I was thinking to myself, "OK, I do not want to be in the position to decide who to sit with if I were to be the last one to grab a tray." Also, as a little social test, I was curious who would choose to sit with ME, as I was the only white man in a large cell area of all black inmates.

I convinced myself, that I HAD to be the FIRST inmate to grab a tray. But I was upstairs and half of the inmates were downstairs. This didn't matter. I HAD to grab the first tray.

I started down the stairs while the guard was still providing instructions. And I walked right up, grabbed the very top tray, and went over to have a seat at one of the steel tables with four stationary seats. Then I waited to see who would sit with me.

I was sitting alone for a while. My table was one of the last tables that were fully occupied. Two others joined me finally. And surprisingly, the two guys who sat with me were the two younger men who were in with me in the first holding cell, H11. They both looked no older than 17 or 18 years old. We sat and we ate breakfast together.

Our discussion was typical "jail talk" at first. As if I knew what typical jail talk was. But our discussion was exactly like what one would imagine jail talk to be. We discussed how crappy the food tastes. One of the young men told us that the food was always terrible. This made me realize at his young age that he has been in jail on more than one occasion. Today the meal was dried up eggs formed like an omelette. We also had sliced apples but they had no taste. In addition, there was some type of potato chunks. They looked like pieces of potato but tasted like a bland semi-soft piece of cardboard. And finally, we had a small cup of orange juice.

We talked about how early they serve breakfast. At this time, it was near 4:30 am. One of the guys told me not to eat too much. Because if I do, you will need to take a crap in the open toilet located in the cell. And nobody likes the thought of taking a dump in the open in front of your cell mates. We talked about the loose jump suits. We talked about the guards being a pain in the butt.

Surprisingly, one of my younger breakfast table mates asked me to talk more about the 401k and the stock market that I touched upon the day before when I was in the holding cell H11. This was when the holding cell H11 was full of men who were saying things like black men don't have anything, so when they get money they go and buy $10,000 wheels. This was when I relayed that my father-in-law had, as a child, less than they do, and that because of that poverty as a youth he invests his money rather than blow his money on wheels and has since amassed a small fortune.

The younger men at my table said they wanted to know more about this. They said they thought it was interesting. So, I spoke about stock. I spoke about e-trade accounts. I spoke about 401k plans. I spoke about IRA's. Not that I am a financial expert, but to them, I was an expert. I was amazed thinking, "Here I was in this notorious Clayton County Jail, and in any jail for the first time in my life, and I am sitting at the breakfast table talking about 401k's, stocks, e-trade and investments, with the hood." They listened intently. They listened very intently and I was very intrigued.

I knew right then that these young men, and probably every other inmate in the jail, had never even heard of these topics. They had no one who could tell them, teach them, or mentor them on finance or investments. All they see are their neighbors, older kids, or gang members buying $10,000 wheels or hitting their WB's. To them, this was an early goal. To be better than the next guy, in their world, one has to buy a better, nicer, more expensive set of wheels, or be tougher on his woman.

It was a somber moment for me. It became more and more apparent to me that many of these young men just don't have the right influences in their lives, or any positive influences, period.

This reminded me of an experience in 1995 when I lived in Dallas, Texas. The company I worked for was developing a new medical office building in Sleepy Hollow, New York. Back then it was called Tarrytown, but they changed the name of the town later to reflect the story of Sleepy Hollow. The little village was located about 45 minutes north of New York City. One of the physicians considering locating to an office in the new building planned for Sleepy Hollow was based in Yonkers, New York. He wanted to meet me in Yonkers instead of Sleepy Hollow.

The administration at the hospital in Tarrytown suggested that I NOT drive to Yonkers due to the high crime in the area. But I checked the maps and the hospital was located less than a half-mile off of the major interstate, Hwy 87. I felt comfortable to drive that half-mile to the hospital campus. Once on campus I thought it would be fairly safe.

I drove from Sleepy Hollow to Yonkers for the meeting. As soon as I took the exit ramp off of Hwy 87, I noticed a stark contrast from what I saw in Tarrytown. I made my left hand turn in the direction of the hospital. There were massive extents of graffiti everywhere. Graffiti was on the buildings. Graffiti was on the cars. Graffiti was on the trees, and even on the sidewalk. Everywhere there was graffiti. There were boarded up windows everywhere in site. On every large building or small house there was plywood over the windows. And on the plywood, there was graffiti.

There were old tires lying in the road. There were burned out shells of cars sitting along the curb. There were old washing machines in the road. There were "thugs" or gang members or nice guys who looked like gang members loitering in small groups on the street corners. As I drove the short distance to the hospital from the highway exit ramp, I saw a little black boy. He was probably eight years old. He had a Dallas Cowboys backpack on. He was apparently walking to school. Yet he was surrounded by all of this graffiti, burned out cars, plywood with graffiti, washing machines, and gang members. This was a sombering moment too.

I thought of my eight-year-old in 1995, who also had a Dallas Cowboys backpack, and who also walked to school. But he was walking past nice families and nice well-kept front yards. My son's walk did not pass by graffiti, or washing machines, or plywood, or gang members.

I thought at that time: "What if I plucked that little eight-year-old boy and brought him back to Dallas and placed him in the same environment as my son and raised with caring parents and neighbors in a nice neighborhood. Would he turn out any differently than his chances are in his environment in Yonkers?" I thought: "This kid really has no chance. All odds are drastically against him."

While I am sitting in the Clayton County Jail eating breakfast at 4:30 am talking about stocks, 401K, and e-trade; and thinking that these young men had seemingly never heard of these things; and that they probably have had nobody in their lives ever who could tell them these things; I thought about that little boy in Yonkers in 1995.

After breakfast, and after the trays were returned to the stack, the inmates in our jail cell area were walking around and having "small talk." We were saying things like, "hey, what's up?"; or "what's happening?" And I see my Memphis friend, the Talker, Reggie. Reggie and I were like "best buddies" by then. He had the MEMPHIS TENNESSEE tattoo in a 120-sized bold new times roman capital letter font on his inner forearms. Reggie was the guy who helped my status grow in the holding cell, when he suggested, with my agreement, that in Memphis they will cut you up for a cigarette.

When I saw Reggie after breakfast, he yelled out, "Yo, Dominic, how's it going man? Are they treating you right in here? Let me know if they don't treat you right!" I went up and tried to do the brothers-handshake-bump and shoulder tap. Hopefully he didn't notice that I had no clue what I was doing. But it was like we were now friends. He had my back. At least that's the way I took it. Reggie, the talker from Memphis, had my back in the Clayton County Jail.

The way the intake progression was structured with the intake waiting room, holding cell H11, then holding cell H12, then the classroom teaching us how to do our mat, towels, and toiletries; then the actual large cell block area; with the same group in each of these progressed areas; allowed us to lukewarmly get to know each other. This was one of the things I thought was nice about the jail. They set it up so by the time you get to your overnight cell, you at least have had a chance meet or have spoken to your future cellmates or colleagues who are all in the large cell bank area. So it avoids a situation where complete strangers are in the cell area. I concluded that this is done deliberately to reduce the potential for conflicts.

HEADED TO THE COURTROOM

After breakfast and after the "socializing," we all went back to our cells, and the central control center locked all the doors. I was still hoping like hell I would see the judge that day. One major problem in jail is that no one tells you anything. You are therefore kind of lost all day. Just waiting for your moment with the judge. I didn't know if my wife secured an attorney or not. I didn't know if my bail had been set. I didn't know if I was being released today.

My moment came near 12:30 pm. The guard rounded us all up and said we were going to see the judge. I was so ecstatic!

We moved from the cell area to the larger

gym-like area. The space was right outside of the jail cellblock area but was a 30 feet tall open space. Almost like a gathering hall. The guards came and told us we were seeing the judge at 1:00 o'clock. They told us that we would walk down a long underground corridor that links the jail to the courthouse.

What they didn't say is that we would be shackled for the walk to and from the courthouse. I was placed in handcuffs, body chains, and foot shackles with chains. This was something I never expected. I was very surprised for my minor offense that I had to be totally shackled like a mass murderer or habitual criminal.

I learned that it was very hard to walk when your feet are chained and shackled. But I was glad my hands were cuffed in front of me instead of cuffed behind my back like they were for the ride from the airport to the jail in the police car. It was very demeaning to be standing there in an orange jumpsuit with chains and shackles, even though every other inmate around me was also in chains and shackles.

We were led out like cattle into the long corridor we had walked down before from holding room H12 to the cell bank. The guards told us to stand against the wall, facing the wall. They announced the "hallway" rules again.

"There will be no talking."

"There will be no running."

"You all will stay in a single file line."

"If a female comes down the hallway, we will immediately turn and face the wall."

"Is that clear?"

We all said, "Yes, sir," in agreement.

We began our walk. This corridor seemed to have no end. You couldn't see the end of the hallway. It was something like 300 yards long. There were 22 inmates, all in orange jumpsuits, all in chains and shackles, all walking in a straight single-filed line.

We were all the same, except one inmate, me, was white.

We walked and walked and walked. It was more like a shuffle than a walk because we couldn't take a normal step with the foot shackles on. We all took baby steps for 300 yards. Twenty-two men in orange jump suits waddling in a single file line down an endless corridor. It was actually a very humorous scene.

Before we were taken to the judge's chamber, we are all crammed into a small room, similar in size to one of the original holding cells. The room is lined with a stainless-steel bench on all walls except a small break in the bench to accommodate a stainless-steel toilet in the corner of the room. Many of us took turns there taking a leak.

I never contemplated in my life that I would be taking a public piss while in handcuffs and shackles surrounded by 21 other grown men in shackles. Taking a wiz was actually easier than one would think. I knew now why the hands were cuffed in the front instead of the back. I am sure the guards don't want to be forced to helping guys taking a leak.

The "watchman" of this area was a black female guard who yelled a lot. She was wide and short and was a tough talker. Her hair was long but unkempt. Her voice was loud but not very legible. Here she was asking us if we had a lawyer or not. We were asked to complete a form about two pages long with several questions.

What is our plea, guilty or innocent?

Do we have a lawyer?

If not, do we want a court appointed lawyer to be assigned?

I had somewhat befriended my cellmate, the older looking gentleman who had to sleep on the floor of my cell. He had become a mentor of sorts because he had been in the jail before and he had coached me on a few things, like don't eat too much, saying, "What goes in has to come out."

He couldn't hear the guard, so he asked her what she said. She glared over at him but gave no answer. The older man raised his hand and asked again, what she had said. He then walked up to her to ask again what she had said.

She then yelled at the top of her lungs, "Shut up, old man, I will add another day to your time!" He grumbled back to her another comment that no one could understand because he said it very low. She then yelled even louder and stronger, "I told you to shut up and sit down!"

The old man scampered back in his shackles to sit next to me and told me, "This is how they treat you in jail. The guards mistreat you, treat you with no respect, yell at you, and taunt you. Then if you say anything back, they really come down on you. They threaten to add days to your time or dish out other punishment like cleaning or cooking." He told me that the whole jail set up is a racket. They encourage you to do something in retaliation so the guards can add a day or two.

He also reminded me the aspect of more man-days equals more money from the state.

In the holding cell before we see the judge, we are filling out the forms with plastic Bic ink pens they had provided us. Trying to hold the pen and the paper form while writing, with no desk, while in handcuffs is very hard to do. I was able to complete my form to let them know that I plead guilty and that I did have an attorney. I turned the paperwork in and sat back down.

We all sat for probably another half-hour. The group had more small talk amongst each other. I again was trying to just sit back and zone out, because I wanted to focus on what the hell I am going to say to the judge. I had never been in front of a judge in my life. I just thought and wondered.

"Will my attorney be there?"

"What will he say?"

"Can I speak to my attorney ahead of time?"

"What should I say?"

"How much is my bail going to be?"

"Will I even get bail?"

"How do you pay the bail?"

"Will I be forced to stay another night in this place?"

"Would I be sentenced for two weeks more?"

"Who would be in the courtroom from my family or friends?"

I knew none of the answers to these questions. So, I sat there in the quietness of my own head, eyes closed, focusing on all these questions, potential answers, and scenarios. I had no clue of what would happen next or what the outcome could be. I was scared.

When the guards came to get us all to take us to the judge's courtroom, they unlocked the door to the holding cell and asked us to step out into the corridor. We were told to stand against the concrete block wall, facing the wall. They then frisked us. I was wondering then why would they frisk us. We had been in the cell the night before, we were all in handcuffs and shackles, we walked down the 300 yard corridor, we were all sitting in the holding cell for an hour. How could we possibly hide something on our body or our cavities? They frisked us none-theless.

As I waited for the others to be frisked, I was standing right next to Reggie. Reggie was the talker. He was the man with the funny stories about his "WB." While standing in the hall next to Reggie, he started cracking more jokes. He joked about the mean woman guard. Reggie talked more about his women. He made wisecracks to the guards and he and they laughed. And I laughed.

I told Reggie that he should go to a comedy club and do an act. He looked at me like I was nuts. He said, "Really?"

I said, "Yeah, man. You are hilarious. That's how Jeff Foxworthy got started and he is the highest earning comedian in history."

I told him how Jeff Foxworthy worked at IBM while he kept his friends and colleagues laughing all day at work. One of his friends told him he should go to the comedy club. After a while trying to convince him, he finally agreed and went to a comedy club in Atlanta. He was a huge hit. After he was invited to be on the Tonight Show he skyrocketed to amazing success and wealth.

I told Reggie he could do the same. I told him he was personable, funny, and charismatic, and that he would create a huge following. I told him to do it. I am not sure if he ever did but he acted like he may consider it after he was released from jail.

Once all the inmates in our group were frisked, we continued our walk, which led us quickly into a small dark elevator lobby. This is where we all, four inmates at a time, took an elevator ride up one floor level and into a small anteroom. The elevator had a guard as an elevator operator. I wondered, what a job! The job tasks are to sit on a stool in a darkened small lobby in the basement level of the courthouse, doing nothing but operating the elevator. I had to assume that the guards are rotated regularly to liven it up a bit. I wondered what their county pay was. I wondered what their county retirement was.

I was told upon exiting the elevator that since I had an attorney he would be in the courtroom and that we would meet up after seeing the judge in a small room divided by glass with a telephone on each side of the glass. We would then talk about next steps and how to get released.

THE COURTROOM

As the single file line continued towards the court-room in the back hallways, I was impressed by the system "behind the scenes" that the public never sees. The hallways, elevators, staff rooms, and dark corridors are all hidden from the average citizen who visits a courtroom. It was like a whole other world. The big courtroom door slightly opens and I immediately see the dark stained mahogany walls through the half opened door, which is about 10 people ahead of me. We all proceed to walk into the courtroom.

The guard in the courtroom that took over the lead from the guard in the corridor is firmly telling everybody, "Do not look towards the back of the courtroom. Is that clear? DO NOT look towards the back of the room, ALWAYS face the judge!."

But one cannot help but to look to the back. We are all wondering who came to see you in court and who is in the room.

I was wondering, "Is my wife there? Is my good friend Bob there? Is my daughter there? Is my older son there? Is my 13-year-old son there? Who else is in the room?" But I could NOT look back.

At this moment, for the first time in my ordeal, I got teary-eyed. I forced myself not to cry but could not refrain from getting teary-eyed. No one that has ever known me has ever seen me in an orange jump suit. No one who has ever known me has ever seen me in handcuffs. No one who has ever known me has ever seen me with my ankles shackled.

I was embarrassed and I was ashamed.

As I entered the courtroom, although forced to not look to the rear of the room, we were facing an area where the attorneys sit. This area was immediately to the right of the judge in front of the room and immediately in front of us as we enter. A black man was sitting in one of the chairs reserved for the attorneys. He had a very nice suit on, he was very tidy, and he was very slick. He looked like a GQ model and just plain cool. He looked right at me, smiled, and waved at me.

I was thinking why is this guy who I never met smiling at me and waving at me. He kept waving and he kept smiling. He stared at me the entire time

I walked in the room and as I navigated to where I would sit.

The guards had all 22 men come in at once. We filled up an entire long bench seat in the front of the courtroom facing the judge. Then we filled up the next row until that was full, then we skipped down to the next row until all in our group were seated, and all facing the judge. I was in the third row of four full rows. Only our group of 22 men were before the judge. It struck me again how organized the movement of inmates was. This is the same group from our very first holding cell, before the jumpsuits and before the sleeping cell, and before breakfast. We all knew each other even in the mildest sense. We were not total strangers.

As I looked at the other inmates it occurred to me that the African American man who was smiling at me and waving at me when I entered the room, had to be my attorney. Having never met him I wondered how he knew that I was his client. Out of 22 people how would he know immediately that I specifically was his client causing him to wave at me?

After more thought, the obvious answer came to mind. I was the white guy. Out of 22 men, I was the ONLY white man. He likely assumed my wife was white by the sound of her voice on the phone. So he assumed I was her husband because I was white. And his assumption was correct.

The judge ordered the inmates to come to the podium one at a time. If they had an attorney, the attorney would join the inmate on the stand. The judge reviews the charges, takes your plea, then relays the court date and states the amount of the bail. I listened and the judge spoke to each inmate ahead of me. I heard charges of racketeering, domestic violence, drug offenses, and more drug offenses. I heard $100 bail, $2,500 bail, and $50,000 bail.

And then it was my turn.

When my name was called, I managed to squeeze out of the row I was in and waddle up to the podium. My attorney joined me. The judge described that my charge is carrying a weapon in an unauthorized location. My plea is guilty. My court date is one month out. My bail is $5,000.

My attorney is the only one to speak. He requested to the judge since this was my first offense, that my bail be reduced to $2,500. The judge immediately denied the request for a bail reduction. My attorney said, "OK, thank you, your honor."

I wondered, "What do I need an attorney for?" I thought that I could have asked this and been denied in the same fashion. And that was that. Very quick concise and we were done. The entire time before the judge was probably less than two minutes.

BACK TO THE CELL

Immediately after we were before the judge, each inmate exits the courtroom one at a time. I exited the courtroom, never looking to the rear. But as I was walking out of the room the guard stopped me and said I need to sign something and to step back in to sign it. When I turned around, I accidentally looked to the rear of the courtroom. One would think I had pulled a gun or something.

The guard yelled, "I TOLD YOU NOT TO LOOK BACK! WHY ARE YOU LOOKING BACK?! ARE YOU MESSING WITH ME?!"

I meekly told him, "I know but y'all called me back and I accidently looked back, geeze!" And I thought about the older cellmate who said it is standard for the guards to yell and taunt the inmates to try and get them to overreact, so they can add a day or two. I signed my form in handcuffs and shackles and left the courtroom.

To my surprise, even though we walked to the courtroom as a group of 22 in a single filed line; after seeing the judge each inmate left the courtroom and walked back to the cellblock area alone. I left the courtroom alone, entered the elevator alone except for the elevator operator, exited the small dark elevator lobby below, and began my trek down the 300 yard long corridor back to my cell block.

While walking, although alone, I could see others who were also alone, but 20, 30 and 40 yards ahead of me. As we walked, I noticed some of the inmates walked faster than others. Some were walking very slowly, maybe to enjoy their "freedom" of not being holed up in a cell with a cellmate, or maybe walking slowly to avoid being in a crowded cell bank area, or just to simply enjoy a leisurely stroll alone.

But for me, I wanted to get back in my cell as soon as possible to lay back on the cot, not talk to anyone, have my wife pay my bail and get the hell out of there as soon as possible. So I was doing something like Charlie Chaplin on steroids; shuffling in shackles as fast as I could down this long wasteland of a corridor. As I was booking it in my orange oversized jump suit, with handcuffs and foot shackles on, I noticed a man in front of me, about 50 feet ahead, who was in a red jump suit, with more chains than me and more shackles than me. He was walking much slower than me, but not by choice.

As we walked, I was "gaining" on him. With each step I took I got closer and closer and closer. This man was shorter than me. I am 6'0" tall and this young man was maybe 5'7" tall. He was very dark toned and stocky. I gained on him and I got right beside him. As we shared 10 – 15 steps together, he glanced up at me to his right side. His eyes were as big as ping-pong balls and as white as the clouds. He looked at me as if he recognized me.

I asked, "Hey man, how's it going?"

As he looked up at me with those big white eyes, he asked me, "Hey man, aren't you that airport gun dude?"

As I chuckled inside, I realized, "Man, I have now made a name for myself here in jail."

I told him, "Yeah, I am the airport gun dude from Memphis, and don't ever forget it!"

I felt somewhat proud actually. I am a man who has never been arrested, have never seen a judge, have always have had a nice career and family, but was now a known figure in the Clayton County Jail.

I was now, "the airport gun dude!"

I continued down the long narrow corridor to my large cellblock, which was the very last block on the left-hand side of the dark hallway. Once I arrived there the guard in the cellblock area finally removed my handcuffs and my foot shackles. I was then able to walk into the large open area of the first floor of the jail cellblock we were in. This was the area where the metal tables and chairs were and where the bank of pay phones was located.

I immediately wanted to call my wife to let her know the bail was $5,000, to ask her to go to the bank, withdraw the money, come back down and get me out ASAP! I absolutely could not wait. At this time, it was around 2 PM. I am thinking I should be out around 3 PM. I was wrong. It was much later.

I went to the phone bank, dialed my wife and an automated voice came on outlining that the call is $15.00 per minute and the receiver of the call must agree to take the call and to pay the charges as a collect call. My wife answered the phone. In order to answer she had to agree to the charges. I told her the bail was $5,000, which she already knew because she was in the courtroom that I couldn't look to the rear of. She said she would go straight to the bank, withdraw the $5,000, come back down to the jail, pay the bail, and get me out. MAN, was I a happy camper!

I then called my daughter and she answered and I and told her. I called my brother and he answered, and I told him. And I called my friend and he answered, and I told him. So, I was set, man. Boy, was I set!

Before I hung up the phone, I noticed a few men standing behind me. There were 6-8 phones, but a line was behind only me, the only white man. I turned to the shorter man in his twenties who was right behind me.

He asked me if he could use the phone. I said, yeah in just a second.

He stopped me and asked, "But can I use it like right now?"

I said, "Just a second."

And he tapped me and said, "I mean now."

He said to me, "I don't have any way to make a call. I don't know nobody with a credit card or a debit card. I don't know nobody with a house phone who can pay for a collect call."

I became very somber again. I was humbled to remember that not all people have what I have.

Some people don't have thousands of dollars in the bank. Some people don't have friends or family with multiple debit cards and credit cards to take a call. Some people don't have friends or family that can easily receive a collect call because they can afford it, or they have the credit for it, or they have a hard-line phone for it. Some people, including the ones right here beside me in jail who can't WAIT to call their family or friends to tell them what their bail is or when their court date is, can't even make a damn telephone call.

I realized that, I, the airport gun dude, am in a small way, their conduit to getting out of this place.

So I kept the telephone line open, I stepped aside, and I allowed several complete stranger, ghetto-hood, drug-addicted men, to use my pre-paid telephone line so they could make their calls. And I was happy to do so and to pay for it.

I was astounded by the fact that that the company who runs the bank of jail phones charges $15.00 per minute and collect calls only.

I wondered, "Why is this so?"

Why make it HARDER for the inmates to call their family immediately after seeing the judge? Why charge $15.00 per minute, the most expensive phone call in the country? Why not allow the free call that we all hear on TV and news? Why make it so difficult to contact people who can help you get out?

The opinion of my cellmates that the jail, or any jail, is set up as a racket came to mind again. I realized the aspect of the state paying some dollar amount per man-day to the county based on jail occupancy is a huge business. The incentive is to keep these men in jail, rather than out of jail. The jail makes it hard for the inmates to get along with the guards. They make it hard for inmates to make a telephone call. Most of the guys in my cellblock were picked up for the most minute drug offense, even if they are a working dad trying to raise a family.

The system is AGAINST these guys.

The system WANTS them there.

The system wants to KEEP them there.

I left the phone bank and went to my cell. I laid down on my cot with my head on my little wadded up hand-towel pillow. And I just laid there.

I thought about how the attorney knew me. I thought about what did the short man who called me "the airport dude" when I was walking back from the judge, do to deserve the red jump suit with double the chains and shackles that I had.

I wondered why they make it hard for the basic urge to call someone harder than it has to be. I wondered if my hair was combed before the judge. I wondered if anyone would enter my cell uninvited. I wondered what time I would get out. I wondered if my wife spoke to my attorney again. I wondered if I would lose my job. I thought about when I would trade the older man my crocs for his flip-flops so that his toes wouldn't hurt.

There were no books. There was no television. There was no iPad, or iPhone. There were no games. There was nothing but an empty cell.

A cell with two cots hung on the wall and a small shelf for our "stuff." And there was an open toilet in the corner. That was it. There was nothing to do but lay there.

So I laid there.

I thought again about when will I get out. It couldn't come quick enough. I thought about how stupid I was taking the damn gun to the airport. I thought about my children, would they be embarrassed.

I thought about my little son who left me the tearful voice mail, would he be afraid I would never come back home. I thought about the little ants in the cell at the airport. Did they ever make it out?

I wondered where my iPad was that was in my bag at the airport but not in the bag when I checked into the jail. I wondered if anyone would notice I was commando in a jumpsuit four times too big, with a long slit down my right side.

I tried to sleep.

MY TIME CAME

Near 9 pm the guards suddenly automatically opened all of the cell doors at once. We were ordered to stand outside our cells and face the control area. A flashlight shown into my eyes and was flickering back and forth.

I wondered, "Why in the hell is this guy flashing the light back and forth into my eyes?"

I asked my cellmates, "What's up with this guy?."

They told me that it was my time to go. I asked, "To go?"

They said, "Yeah, get yo stuff and get on outta hea." They told me to grab my sheets and blanket, my washcloth, and my sleeping pad, and my big plastic tub and get out of the room. They said I was free to go.

I have never moved so quickly in my life. I

grabbed "my stuff." I grabbed the towel, the washrag, the sleeping pad, the blankets, and tossed them into my tub and hit the door. Just as I began to walk down the stairs, a guard on a loud speaker yelled, "EVERYBODY STAND STILL! WE KNOW YOU HAVE A GUN STASHED IN THERE SOMEWHERE AND WE WILL FIND IT!"

I thought, "Oh my god, now it is my time to leave and now I have to get that cavity search I feared so they can look for a gun hidden in a body part." But the dude in the control area outside our cellblock, with the flashlight, kept waving it into my eyes. I now knew that this meant for me to keep walking and that I was being asked to leave. I walked down the stairs through the large open dining and common area on the first floor level and up to the big glass doors that separated the cellblock areas from the central control area. As I went to open it, it was still locked.

In the meantime it was getting more and more chaotic in the cell area, where the guards were screaming that, "WE WILL FIND THIS DAMN GUN!"

I thought, "Get me out of here as soon as possible man."

The guards kept screaming and searching and I kept waiting and waiting for what seemed to be 15 or 20 minutes but was likely more like 2-3 minutes.

As I waited staring directly at the control guard who can unlock the door electronically, and waiting for him to do so, a middle-aged man came up to me.

He asked me, "Are you being let out?"

I told him, "Yes, I was being let out, finally!"

He asked me, "What is your bail?."

I told him, "My bail was $5,000 and my wife brought it down and got me out."

He looked to the ground with a sad face and proceeded to say, "My bail is $100."

I asked him why he isn't getting out and he said, "I don't have anybody in my world who can pay $100. So I have to stay in here for three months until my court date."

I felt extremely bad at that moment. I thought, "My wife can go to the bank and take out $5,000, drive to the Clayton County Jail, pay my bail and get me out with no problem." Yet this man, whose bail is only $100, has no one, not a single soul, who can stop by and pay his $100 bail to get him out of this place. Although I felt really bad, I was only thinking about my getting out. And all I wanted to do at that moment was to get out.

Amazingly, the door was still locked. I stood there with my large bucket of all my jail possessions right at the glass doors and waited. The man with the $100 bail walked away with his head down, and another man approached me.

Willie was a clean-cut man with a nicely trimmed beard and maybe 45 years old. He asked, too, if I was getting out. I almost said, "No I am just standing here with all my stuff at the big glass door to await a cavity search for the gun." But I didn't. I just told him, "Yeah I am getting out." He told me his wife will not get him out and his neighbors will not get him out. He said he really wants out and that he had a friend who would get him out. He asked if I would be willing to call his friend when I got to the other side, to see if he could get him out of jail.

There were no pens or pencils in this area of the jail because they could be used as a weapon. There was no way to write down a telephone number, or a name, or an address. I could only ask him what his friend's name was. I learned many years before that if you heard something three times in a row it would be retained for life. I told him to tell me his friend's name. He told me his name and that he owned a used car dealership in Lawrenceville, GA, in Gwinnet County. He told me his friend's name again and where he worked. He told me his friend's name again and where he worked. I asked him one more time and he told me his friend's name and where he worked.

I then promised Willie I would make the call

and I would get him out of jail. As he walked away, he was smiling from ear to ear.

He trusted me.

As the glass door unlocked, I immediately felt free. I walked out of the glassed-in cellblock area and into the central large open area where the control center was. I was instructed to place my tub on the floor and to go ahead and walk out. The simplicity of release was surprising, given the complexities of the check in process and visiting the judge.

The walk out route was to leave the central hub area and into the long corridor. The same 300 yard corridor that we walked in a single filed line to see the judge earlier in the day. I was unexpectedly totally alone in the entire hallway this time. There were no guards. There were no other inmates. It was only me in an extremely long 12-foot wide dark windowless corridor.

As I walked, I thought. I thought about the young man with the $100 bail, who would be forced to spend three months in jail for his court date, for probably a minute drug offense. I thought about Reggie the talker, and if he was still telling hilarious stories with his cellmates.

I thought about the guards who generally

mistreated all the regular inmates. I thought about how my attorney knew that I was his client without ever seeing me before. I thought about the older cell mate of mine who told me his thong flip flops really hurt his feet because he had to keep his thick white socks on.

I suddenly remembered that I promised him that I would trade my crocs for his flip slops when I was released so his feet wouldn't hurt. I thought about turning back, but I couldn't. I thought about my kids, my wife, my job, my family, and my freedom. I just couldn't turn back just to swap shoes with another inmate, although I promised him that I would.

What would the guards say? What would the check-out person think if I was leaving with different shoes than what were given to me at check in? Would this cause an issue or delay in my being released? I thought again about turning back and trading shoes, but I concluded it was too risky, so I did not do so.

I thought about what my older cellmate thought. I wondered if he thought I was a bad person for not following through with my promise I made to him. I thought about how many more days or weeks his feet would have to hurt him. I felt bad. But I kept walking to my own freedom.

I reached the end of the long hallway and wasn't sure where to go. I did see a small check-in window.

I approached the window and told them that I was told I could leave. The clerk asked me my name and they proceeded to look for my bag of clothes and possessions they took from me when I checked in the day before. They gave me the large clear bag with all of my clothes and the piece of paper that we had to fill out when we changed into the jumpsuit. They asked me to step into a small dressing room to change out of my orange jumpsuit and into my street clothes.

I couldn't wait to take off the jumpsuit and I did. I put on my dress shirt, my dress pants, my black socks, my dress shoes, and my belt. Then I placed the suit coat on. I retrieved from another bag my wallet, my pens, and, yes, my coveted Chapstick. I walked back up to the little window to give them my jumpsuit, which I placed in the same clear bag. The attendant took the bag, pressed a buzzer that unlocked the door, and she asked me to go ahead and leave.

FREEDOM

My wife was in a small waiting area and waited for me to come to her. We hugged and I was happy. And she was happy.

My first stop was to another window clerk area where I was given back my money, which was removed from my wallet when I checked in. They take all money to make sure it isn't stolen in jail. The cash was documented at check in and the inmate is asked to sign the form that verified all possessions.

Our good friend drove my wife down to the jail and he joined us outside for the hour and a half drive home. I talked and talked all the way home. We laughed and laughed. Bob couldn't believe I had such a good time in jail. He was expecting the worst, but my experience was very different than what he expected and from what I expected.

When we arrived home my family was relieved to see that I actually made it out of the slammer and was not raped. We hugged and laughed and talked. And, man, did we talk.

I told the stories of Reggie, the talker. I told the story of the African castle, the singing in H12, and the commando confession.

I told the story of the investments, 401K, of the bad food, the sassy guards, and the old man who asked to trade our shoes.

I told the story of the "gay Michael Jackson" dude above me on the top cot, and of the old man sleeping on the floor of our cell.

I told the story of how I actually learned a lot by being in the jail, and that really it was a very interesting experience.

After a day or two of dwelling on the experience further and sharing my ordeal with friends and family, I thought about Willie, the gentleman who asked me as I was about to leave, to call his buddy to get him out. Remember, there were no pens to write anything down, but from memory, I recalled that Willie's friend had an upscale used car dealership in Lawrenceville, GA and I remembered the name of the dealership. So, I called.

I spoke not directly with Willie's friend, but to Willie's friend's wife. I said, "Hello, this is a jailmate of one of your friends and he asked that I call you to get him out because he said his wife won't get him out."

She said, "Oh, man, is he in jail again?" She asked what he was in for and I told her I wasn't sure, but Willie was sure you guys could get him out. She said, reluctantly, that she and her husband would get him out. I told her I really appreciated it. Why I appreciated it, I don't know. I just know that Willie, as I did, would want to get out of the hellhole.

Through my research of the jail, Clayton County Courts, and the county court clerk's office, I learned by accident that there is an online database that shows all arrestees and who are listed as a current "resident" of the Clayton County Jail. I checked it and it still showed me as a resident, which highly concerned me. Because I thought if my company ever saw this I am screwed royally. My listing was removed about two days later, so I was good.

Upon further research, I did find that Willie was listed as well. Since he was listed, I knew that I could go back to make sure he was released, with the help of his used-car-dealer friend. So I checked it daily. After about three days I went to the online database and found that he had been released.

Surprisingly, it left me with a big blanket of satisfaction. As if I owed it to Willie. I gave him my word and I followed up with my word. I didn't know Willie at all. Never even met him in jail, before the

time he walked up to me as I was about to be released from the cell block and asked me call his
friend. But I gave him my word, and I know he had
the same discomfort in jail as me. He had the same
uncertainty as I had. He couldn't wait to get out, as I
couldn't wait to be out. He had a wife and he had a
family, too. So I made the call and I got Willie out.

THE FOLLOWING DAYS

After a few more days, I couldn't stop thinking about all these guys at the jail. I thought about how most of the inmates were young, although some were older. I thought about how the vast majority were in there for minor drug offenses. I thought about how the vast majority had no one who could bail them out, even for a $100 bail.

I thought about how many of them would have to sit in jail for weeks or months until their court date came up. I thought about how most had no hope, no family, and no money. I thought about how the young men asked me at breakfast about stocks and 401K's.

I thought about how most of the residents in the Clayton County Jail had no role models or guidance.

I wanted to go back and speak to them. I called

the jail; I called my attorney; and I called the courthouse to find ways where I can go back and talk to these guys about life.

I wanted to talk about how to do good and not bad. I wanted to describe how to invest and not blow $10,000 on wheels. I wanted to talk to them about not beating their WB.

But everywhere I turned, I was told I could not do so. I was told they didn't let those released to come back and talk to the people still locked up. I was told that they don't allow it. After many attempts, I concluded that the system really is a racket. It really is a system where the goal is to maintain maximum occupancy in order to be paid more money by the state. I concluded that the main goal of the county jail, really, is to lock people up for minor offenses for as long as possible.

And to make it as difficult as possible to make a phone call; and to make it as difficult as possible to pay bail; and to make it as difficult as possible to get these guys on a good tract.

In relaying this days later to my wife, I surprisingly cried, and cried, and cried. I somehow felt guilty because I could easily pay my bail, through cash, credit cards, friends and family, while most of the other cellmates couldn't get a $100 bail paid. I felt somewhat guilty because I had a great family with guidance, love and attention, while most of these guys had none of that. They had no guidance, attention, love or teachings about life, money, or women. And how this cycle has and would continue indefinitely.

I wanted to determine what happened to my iPad. It was in my workbag at the airport, but it was not in my bag when I checked into the jail. I knew that somebody had stolen it! My iPad was stolen by the jailer, the cops, or somebody else, I assumed. I had my Apple devices set up to "track iPad" if it were ever lost. I logged on the "find my iPad" site and found that it was still showing to be at the airport! I was thinking, "Airport? What the hell?" Why is my $600 iPad still at the airport several days after I was arrested? I looked up the number to the airport police department. I called the little square cubbie where the police originally talked to me. I called the on-site police department at the airport with the two little cells and I spoke to the overall police department. Of course, no one knew anything about the iPad. So I was now pissed.

On the locator app, you can type a message so that anyone using the device can see the message. I opted to type a message that read, "I know who you are and I know you have my iPad. I also know your location and I will come after you! Please leave it somewhere and I will come and get it."

I waited several minutes and resent the message. Then I waited several hours and re-sent the message. Then a day or two later I resent the message. I received no response whatsoever. Man, was I still pissed?

I am thinking that I am arrested against my will, then someone at the police department decides to steal my iPad. As my anger brewed, I decided to call the airport police department again to let them know it is at the airport, so it has to be at the police department, and I was pissed that someone there stole it from me.

Only then did they advise me, "Oh, yeah, we always take expensive items out of people's bags, like computers, iPads, phones, etc."

I asked, "Why do you do this?"

She said, "To make sure these items are not stolen at the jail."

I felt an appreciation that they at least are watching out for your items to some extent. I asked, "But why do you not tell the arrestee that you took possession of these expensive personal devices and what you did with them?"

She advised that I should have been told. I am then thinking, "Yeah, right. They probably sit unclaimed for weeks and then the police department sees it as "unclaimed property," because the owner has no clue where it is."

When I asked where it is, she said it was now at the central police department personal items department. I asked, "Police department personal property department? What is that?" I learned that it was a huge warehouse, probably 200,000 square feet, in downtown Atlanta where they keep and store all confiscated items. She told me that I had to go down there personally to retrieve the iPad.

I made the 45-minute drive to the warehouse. I went to the reception window, told her my name and presented ID, and lo and behold, after a 45-minute wait, the clerk brings out a nice sealed box with my iPad in it. It was amazing to see that there is an entire infrastructure in the police system that actually works.

In my mind, traditionally, anything run by governments doesn't work or at least not effectively or efficiently. But I was very pleased to have my iPad back in my hands. I left happy.

My next task was to retrieve the gun of my father that my siblings allowed me to have at my father's death. When I checked with the courts and my attorney, they both told me, "Oh, no, you don't get that gun back."

I asked, "Why not?"

They said, "It's part of the punishment for carrying a weapon in an unauthorized location."

I asked both the attorney and the courts, on separate occasions, "Is it legal for me to get and carry a gun?"

And they both said, "Oh, yeah. You can go out and buy a gun tomorrow!"

So of course I asked, "If I can go out and buy a gun tomorrow, why can't I just get my father's gun back?"

I was told, "Because it is a form of punishment."

I told them, "But this was my deceased father's gun. I got it upon his death. It has sentimental value.."

They both said, "Sorry you are not getting the gun back. It will be destroyed."

I was in a funk then. I am thinking, "Oh my god, my father has had this gun for years and I lost it due to being a dumb ass." I wanted to replace the gun from my father. I started searching online for guns like the one I had taken from me. This was a Colt Mustang 380. When I began searching, I find out that the Colt Mustang 380 is not a cheap device. Most guns for sale like this were near $1,500. I knew my dad always had style. Even with his guns he had style. I loved him dearly.

But it occurred to me. The police catch me with a gun at the airport, my bad. Then they realize this is a $1,500 gun and not a $250 gun. So they confiscate it, keep it, and sell it. I don't know if they actually sold it. They told me that all guns confiscated are destroyed to keep them off the streets. But economically that makes no sense. I still suspect that somebody in the police department understood the value of the gun and opted to sell it instead. At least that's what I feel happened. I just can't see them destroying a $1,500 gun.

THE GUN SAFETY CLASS AND COMMUNITY SERVICE

One of the requirements of my release was that I needed to attend a "Gun Safety Class." The Clayton County public attorney did a good job in finding a location near me for the class. The Clayton County Jail is one hour and 30 minutes away, but the gun safety class was only five minutes away from me. The public attorney also attended the gun class. I was fairly impressed. Apparently there are lots of stupid people like me who carry guns through airport security.

In the class, the instructor, who was a deputy in Georgia who teaches this class on the side, mentioned during the class that in Clayton County, all first-time offenders with no record have their offense automatically expunged. I was thinking about the fact that I just paid my attorney $3,500 to expunge my record, so I raised my hand. I asked, "If Clayton County automatically expunges the offense for first time offenders, did I need an attorney in order to expunge my record?"

He said with confidence, "No, you didn't need an attorney. You would have had an expunged clean record whether you had an attorney or not." Now I am pissed again. This attorney clearly took advantage of me. I won't mention any names but if he is reading this book, "I know you screwed me."

During a break in the class, I was speaking with another "student." We were discussing the craziness of it all. We discussed the mistreatment by the guards, the worries, and just stupidity of taking a gun through security. I mentioned something about the food. He immediately said, "I didn't eat any food, man."

I said, "Why not, the bologna sandwich wasn't bad. Bologna on wheat."

He said if you eat you have to crap. And he wasn't about to take a dump on the toilet sitting in the corner of this room with 22 people lining the room sitting on a bench. It was hilarious!

Another requirement of my release was community service. I was asked to come back to the Clayton

County Courts to meet with the court attorney to go over the requirements for community services. I made yet another hour and a half drive down to Clayton County.

In the meeting he advised that my community service requirements are 200 hours helping the community with many non-profit organizations. One organization that is not approved is working with my own church. He had a thick booklet with dozens of organizations that would comply with the community service guidelines.

The court attorney went over Habitat for Humanity, which I thought would be good due to my background in architecture and real estate. He reviewed low-income community centers where I could help out with various projects. He explained in detail several area organizations where I could expend time with underprivileged kids. He introduced me to missions, abuse centers, homeless shelters, and many other groups and activities that would meet the 200-hour requirement.

The attorney was very effective in describing the community benefits and the appreciation that the community and the courts have when help is provided through community service.

I asked again if I could come down and talk to the residents of the jail to teach them big lessons about life, finances, relationships, stay off drugs, etc.

He again said I couldn't do this. I don't understand why this is against the rules because the guys in the jail need help too and I really wanted to do this for my community service. But I was declined.

This meeting was probably at least an hour and 15 minutes long after he outlined all the areas where I could sign up for community service. And I was considering all the options on what to do and what best I could do to help the residents in these communities.

As I was pondering these options, the attorney suddenly mentioned, "Or you could just pay us $150 which will go towards Toys for Tots."

I asked, "Pay $150 for Toys for Tots?"

He said, "Yes that will suffice as your full community service."

I was a bit stunned. He spent so much time that morning describing all the organizations that will help a community, but then he tells me that a check for $150 will meet the requirements too.

I told him, "But I thought community service was actual hours spent helping the community."

He said, "I know, but Toys for Tots will provide toys for the poor children at Christmas. We get a full tractor-trailer rig full of all kinds of toys. And these toys are taken out and given to area children living in poverty that couldn't otherwise have nice toys."

I told him I would just do that then and I wrote my check.

LESSONS

Overall, I have to say going to jail was a really good experience. I learned more than I could ever have otherwise. I actually enjoyed the conversations, the humor, teaching some of the inmates a few things that they may not have ever heard before, and them teaching me a few things I had never realized.

I enjoyed listening to some of the stories relayed by the "hood." I laughed so hard at the "WB" stories. I enjoyed the singing and the jokes and the laughter. It was funny listening to the "jive talk." I felt the emotion when the guys were reflecting on their own lives and personal hardships. I was intrigued with the story about the visit to Africa by one of the inmates.

I learned how difficult it is for these guys to get out of jail or to even make bail, or to make a simple phone call. I enjoyed talking to the guys about money, women, and life. I felt happy when I got Willie out. I learned that most of these men are very nice and kind and they are mostly arrested for menial drug offenses. I am convinced that the jail system is a racket.

I wonder to this day how Reggie is doing; or the electrician, or the younger guys asking me about stocks. I wonder how the old man wearing flip-flops is doing.

Within one year of my "fun" time in jail, in reading the electronic version of the Atlanta Journal Constitution newspaper, I see a story about guns at Atlanta Hartsfield airport. Of course, I couldn't resist reading the story.

To my dismay I read that there are changes to the rules or laws related to those who are caught with a gun in a carry-on bag. Rather than being arrested and spending the night in one of the area's most notorious county jails, like I had to do, the person caught is now allowed to simply take the gun back to his car and then return to catch his flight.

I was thinking, "That's my luck." But I am convinced that my experience may have been one that encouraged the courts to change the gun policy. And I have no problem playing my part in it.

ACKNOWLEDGEMENTS

I never could have written Airport Gun Dude, if my cellmates in Clayton County Jail had not been so welcoming, funny, supportive, and entertaining during my time there. I also want to thank my wife, Wanda, and wonderful children, Danielle, Dante and Vinny, who also encouraged me for several years to write of my experience. And to my remaining siblings, Tina, Ricci (also a writer of poetry), and Mario who all stayed on me to get my story out.

Lastly, I wanted to thank the Babcock Family at Deed's Publishing for believing in me, and in my book, to help reach final publication.

None of this may have happened without everyone's support and encouragement.

Thank you all!

ABOUT THE AUTHOR

Damian Donati is one of five children, where he had the time of his life growing up in a strict but very loving and close Italian family in Germantown, TN. One of his passions is writing, having drafted several books since 1995 about his real life experiences. He includes humor and emotion to his stories hoping to share some of his own fun with his readers.

Damian is also a successful businessman in the commercial real estate niche, having developed medical facilities in 34 states across the country since 1983. He resides in North Georgia with his wife of 37 years, and enjoys lots of cookouts and family time with his three adult children, also in Atlanta, and his first grandchild.

CPSIA information can be obtained
at www.ICGtesting.com
Printed in the USA
LVHW032249280621
691388LV00003B/8